AF291140

THE ART OF DIREMPTION

THE GERMAN LIST

THE ART OF DIREMPTION

On the Powerlessness of Art

LEONHARD EMMERLING

TRANSLATED BY PARNAL CHIRMULEY

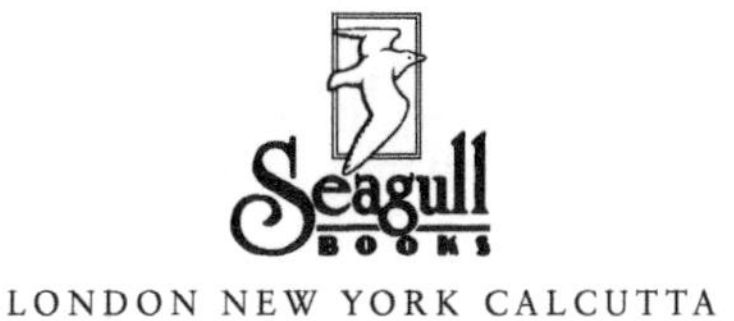

LONDON NEW YORK CALCUTTA

The translation of this work was funded by Geisteswissenschaften International–Translation Funding for Work in the Humanities and Social Sciences from Germany, a joint inititative of the Fritz Thyssen Foundation, the German Federal Foreign Office, the collecting society VG WORT and the Börsenverein des Deutschen Buchhandels (German Publishers and Booksellers Asociation).

Seagull Books, 2021

First published in German as *Kunst der Entzweiung*: *Zur Machtlosigkeit von Kunst* by Leonhard Emmerling © Turia + Kant, 2017

First published in English by Seagull Books, 2021 English translation © Parnal Chirmuley, 2021

ISBN   978 1 8030 9 034 4

British Library Cataloguing-in-Publication Data A catalogue record for this book is available from the British Library.

Typeset by Seagull Books, Calcutta, India Printed and bound in the USA by Integrated Books International

CONTENTS

Introduction

Art pedagogues and exhibition organizers, artists and curators, biennale specialists and theoreticians, and those who shape the discourse in the field of contemporary Western art seem to have two things in common—one, the belief that they play a role in transforming society for the better. And two—the idea that art, especially contemporary visual art, is greatly suited to addressing all manner of social, political, economic, ecological and other imbalances, and to showing consumers of art as well as other members of society the way out of their self-imposed immaturity and blindness.

There is an almost relentless spate of exposures and revelations, interventions and calls to participation, through which boundaries are crossed and conventions broken, social relations unmasked and power equations brought to light, as though everyone but the artist were caught in this cycle of blindness:[1] engagement as a way of not becoming involved. The artist's position as exceptional is similar to that of the prophet. Despite the seeming fondness for the postmodern, it is the enlightenment that is its project, and the dull mass of fools subjected to

---

1 Theodor W. Adorno, *Negative Ästhetik* in *Gesammelte Schriften*, VOL. 6 (Frankfurt am Main, 1970), p. 365.

an endless education is the object of its efforts. This presumptuous heroism can be described as nothing but 'false consciousness',[2] a wilful blindness towards one's subjugation to the contradictions inherent in social relations, the denial of the existence of these contradictions, and in fact the assertion that these can all be solved in the here and now. No matter how unshakeable Adorno's faith may have been in the idea that art can keep the possibility of a reconciliation of these contradictions alive, he also cautioned us that such a reconciliation is not imminent and that art would bereft itself of its legitimacy if it insists that creating a society free of violence is entirely possible if one just knows the trick.

The language of the artist—and that of his disciples—as a privileged seer must necessarily give up on dialectics entirely whereby the prophet is revealed as a philistine who finds ambiguity of any kind revolting. This rhetoric is rooted in avant-gardist modernity and attaches itself seamlessly to a work of art. Habermas' verdict on this work of art and its futuristic, surrealistic and far younger predecessors labouring to amalgamate art and life and expand the definition of art is that they are nonsense experiments.[3]

Nonsense, because there is an economy at play which no one agent will be able to break through. This economy can be described as a cross-financed valorization between morals and

---

2 See Theodor W. Adorno, *Aesthetic Theory* (Robert Hullot-Kentor trans. and introd.) (Minneapolis: University of Minnesota Press, 1997), p. 191 for a discussion on false consciousness: 'Rather, ever since freedom emerged as a potential, correct consciousness has meant the most progressive consciousness of antagonisms on the horizon of their possible reconciliation.'

3 Jürgen Habermas, 'Die Moderne—ein unvollendetes Projekt' (1980) in *Die Moderne—ein unvollendetes Projekt. Philosophisch-politische Aufsätze 1977–1990* (Leipzig: Reclam Bibliothek, 1990), p. 46.

aesthetics. What is valorized is what can otherwise be described as social work, through the context of art, and what gets valorised, is, by way of the morally valuable aim, namely, that of participation, what could at best be referred to as epigonism in the context of art. This cross-financed valorization takes place on the plane of aesthetic difference as the primary distinction between reality and seeming, and must be both negated and affirmed, should an exchange of these values be at all possible.

It is nonsense also because this cross-financed valorization is ultimately directed at a neutralization of one by the other. The aesthetic difference guarantees administrators of public money, who finance participatory interventions in the public space, the absence of facing any consequences arising out of artistic intervention. Thus, they can return to their primary preoccupation, namely, the management of public affairs, possibly with entirely new ideas. Aesthetic difference, on the other hand, guarantees that no one questions the artist about what kind of falsifiable or verifiable results their artistic research (preferably in the 'urban space' at the intersection between gender, public space, and the economy, or something similar) has achieved, nor about what conclusions may be drawn from it. To that extent, such cross-financing ensures the unmitigated coexistence of bureaucracy and art without the slightest whiff of danger that anything could, should or would have to actually change.

The tendency towards the erasure of aesthetic difference at the cost of an amalgamation of art and life—which formerly characterized the avant garde, and which continues to exist in instances of the relational aesthetic, intending to put an end to the lack of consequences in the social realm, which is really its weakness—has not only long ago come to occupy a mainstream position in the art world but also finds its truest realization in economically determined efforts at building a creative economy. Creativity has mutated from being a paradigm of the subject's self-empowerment to a virtue of the flexible entrepreneur intentionally serving every changed circumstance in the labour market. The idea of the creative potential of every subject has in a sense come true, in ways that even Joseph Beuys would never have thought possible. Individual subjects may not come together to create a different society; rather, it is the market that, in a post-Fordist and post-disciplinary society, both steers and commands the subject's creative potential so as to enable her to place it at the service of the economy. From that perspective, the high status accorded to art in Western society—and the numbers of visitors to museums speak volumes—is no indicator of the appreciation of art but, rather, of the commodification of art. Taste and awareness of 'relevant' phenomena is a currency that proves to be of great value to the consuming subject in her struggle for the most subtly balanced use of cultural capital and the acquisition of finer distinctions.[4] Accordingly, the status of the artist (whether symbolic or in terms of prices) who serves the demands of the respective markets is higher. This is not the market of the collector alone; it is also the market of the art-savvy administration that is well aware of the importance of art as a locational advantage which artists suitably serve under the label of contextual specificity.

The assumption that art has a unique ability to bring truth to light possibly underlies the soteriological certainty that art can change the world for the better. This assumption is only possible as long as one believes that art is not the same as seeming. Truth, after all, cannot be illusory. In order to resolve

---

4 See Christoph Menke, 'Ästhetische Freiheit: Geschmack wider Willen' (2009) in *Die Kraft der Kunst* (Berlin: Suhrkamp Verlag, 2013), pp. 132–49.

this conflict between the claim of art to truth and its status as illusion, art has, for over a hundred and fifty years, strived to counter the idea of itself. Today, art is what subverts the idea of art. It is persistent about disencumbering itself of its seemingly illusory character in order to become a part of reality, and to attempt, in that capacity, to have a transformative impact. This requires a consensus on the status of this reality. For this reason, art that seeks to be transformative appeals to a community. It is not, as in the case of Rilke, the individual subject who trembles at the invocation by the stone that she must transform her life.[5] Rather, it is the communitized subject who, with other subjects, works towards changing the world for the better. Art thus serves as a model for a successful social existence, and it is only from this that art draws its relevance.

The subjective, aesthetic judgement does not suffice in the formation of a community that is approaching a future of salvation. From the aesthetic judgement by the individual of a given work must emerge cognitive judgement, which finds the proof of the correctness of its results and possible consequences in the correspondence of thought with its objects and in the consistency of the subjective will with the collective will of the community. Moral judgement, which claims normativity, places itself above the aesthetic which has no objective purpose and therefore no normative power. Aesthetic judgement is the same as the pretentious, elite evaluation of a work of art as beautiful. There is little that is less relevant than beauty. Its historic status[6] is that of deceptive and illusory appearance.

---

5 Rainer Maria Rilke, 'Archaischer Torso Apollos' (1908), in *Sämtliche Werke*, VOL. 1 (Frankfurt am Main: Insel Verlag, 1955), p. 557.

6 See Christoph Menke, 'Die Macht der Schönheit: Überlegungen zu ihrem geschichtlichen Stand' in Michael Krüger (ed.), *Was ist noch schön an den Künsten?* (Göttingen: Wallstein, 2015), pp. 103–27.

The conflict between truth and seeming corresponds to the conflict between aesthetic judgement, which is necessarily subjective, and the claim of art, which seeks to offer objective analyses of and intervene in and transform real life. Herein lies the reason that it waives autonomy and maintains a claim to being research.[7] Autonomy is renounced in every form of relational art, in every form which embodies an extended definition of art. What is at stake is to have an impact and to exert power in the realm of the heteronomous.

The devalorization of aesthetic judgement corresponds to the increasing valorization of moral judgements. The aesthetic insignificance of a large proportion of contemporary art has to be offset by moral relevance, through the social 'impact' that, in an economy of value, occupies first place along with the value of the symbolic capital of art.

What morality may have to say to art, and which arguments it uses to do so in order to assess the relation of art to society is a concern for the praxis of observation that seeks to clarify when the intervention of morality is morally justified. The ethics of the aesthetic observes how the aesthetic interacts with its relation to society. It does not generate a morality out of this observation. However, it does evaluate the ways in which society assesses the consequences of the aesthetic differentiation between reality and seeming, that is, aesthetic difference, the flaw of the lack of social consequences. Aesthetics observes the ways in which art processes such a differentiation. The prerogative of ethics is to observe whether the aesthetic communicates with society appropriately and meaningfully.

---

7 For a discussion on the modest level at which the discourse on art as research is conducted, see Dieter Mersch, *Epistemologien des Ästhetischen* (Zürich: Diaphanes, 2015).

❀

INTRODUCTION

In understanding Kant's definition of aesthetic judgement as being reflective, and in outlining a brief history of how it has been hollowed out, the intention behind the following chapters is not to hold up a normative definition of the aesthetic, of beauty, to contemporary art, and to critique it from that vantage point. The greater concern is to arrive at a conception of what art can and cannot achieve within society. It is the indefatigability of doubt,[8] of uncertainty about the self, of thought and analysis that questions itself, and does not let itself be transformed into a cognitive judgement. Aesthetic judgement in its reflexivity is unable to rid itself of its weakness. It thus corresponds with its object. Art is weak. It therefore requires an ethics of powerlessness, which rejects the discourse of impact and power, in order to enable a politics of art, at the heart of which lies the permanence of reflection, unfoundability of thought and the emergence of form as the event of the new.

---

8 On the role of doubt in René Descartes, see Hannah Arendt, '*Vita activa oder Vom tätigen Leben*' (1958) (Munich, Berlin: Piper Verlag 2016), p. 348. For a more positive engagement with the question of doubt, see Sundar Sarukkai, 'To Question and not to Question: That is the Answer' in Romila Thapar, with Sundar Sarukkai, Dhruv Raina, Peter Ronald DeSouza, Neeladri Bhattacharya and Jawed Naqvi, *The Public Intellectual in India* (New Delhi: Aleph, in association with The Book Review Literary Trust, 2015), pp. 41–62; here, p. 44.

Kant I

> It is plain that the Beautiful, the judging of which has
> at its basis a merely formal purposiveness, that is, a pur-
> posiveness without purpose, is quite independent of the
> concept of the Good; because the latter presupposes an
> objective purposiveness, that is the reference of the
> object to a definite purpose.[1]

Purposiveness without purpose and disinterested pleasure
together form the basis of Kant's judgement of beauty. The formal purposiveness of the work of art at its inception corresponds to the disinterestedness at the stage of its reception. The
absence of any particular interest, any private tendency, any
individual admixture of charm and a stirring of emotions[2] in
the perception of the beautiful,[3] explains why the observer can
presuppose that the pleasure that she feels in this observation
becomes 'a ground of satisfaction for everyone'.[4] The judgement

---

1 Immanuel Kant, *Critique of Judgement* (James Creed Meredith trans.)
(Oxford: Oxford University Press, Oxford World Classics, 2007[1952]), p. 44.

2 Kant, *Critique of Judgement*, §13, p. 43.

3 Kant, *Critique of Judgement*, §6, pp. 33–4.

4 Kant, *Critique of Judgement*, §6, p. 33.

based on taste is in fact 'not a judgement of cognition, and is consequently not logical but aesthetical, by which we understand that [...] its determining ground can be no other than subjective'.[5] However, because whoever finds something beautiful, has reason to 'impute' a similar satisfaction to others, the judgement of taste must be bound to its claim to subjective universality.[6]

The nature of judgement of the beautiful as a result of reflective judgement[7] (as opposed to a definitive one) holds this judgement in abeyance, and there is no way to transform this into a judgement based on reason. Paired with disinterestedness and finding expression in reflexive judgement, it is that very subjectivity, which is a prerequisite for imputing a universal sense and for the hope of agreement by others (ideally, by all others), that seems at all justified. The need to examine reflective judgement by holding it up to all of human reason[8] shapes the collective sense, which is a result of a self-doubting reflection that at the same time examines this doubt, that is, the consideration for the judgement of others.

The subject can, on the one hand, be certain, that her judgement follows a certain set of rules that can also be applied to others. What separates the subject from [all] others—her subjectiveness—is the most general attribute that she nevertheless shares with other subjects. The subject distances herself from her particular interests nearly to the point of total transparency in the aesthetic judgement as disinterestedness. In this judgement that is based on nothing other than her *own* subjectivity,

---

5 Kant, *Critique of Judgement*, §1, p. 27.

6 Kant, *Critique of Judgement*, §6, p. 34.

7 Kant, *Critique of Judgement*, §44, p. 110–11.

8 Kant, *Critique of Judgement*, §40, p. 102.

the subject becomes apparent to her own subjectivity as disinterested and as free of all particular agreements.

However, this form of judgement as entirely reflective is a cause for enduring doubt—it appears to not be based on information that can be empirically substantiated. It is the permanence of reflection as permanence of doubt that corresponds to the division between the isolation of the subject and the universality of the division that binds all subjects together.

In this interminable shift from subjectivity to generalization, from subjective generalization and generalization about the subject, lies the explanation for the appeal of aesthetic judgement to human rationality to evoke trust in subjective judgement and produce general intelligibility. Such a *sensus communis* evolves not so much from an agreement on verifiable facts but, rather, from a discursive comparison, a reflective engagement with the uncertainty that is rooted purely in the subjective and is in that sense an entirely general uncertainty.[9]

The 'purposiveness without purpose' as aesthetic purposiveness to which disinterested pleasure corresponds, represents the validity of judgement in its freedom.[10] The freedom of judgement corresponds to the freedom that the work, in its autonomy, determines, establishes, reveals and exemplifies as a purely formal purposiveness. The work itself is the only embodiment of the validity of the laws it follows and its purposiveness, which explains why judgement, insofar as it correlates with the work, is a pure formulation of the freedom as well as the validity of [reflective] judgement. Since the given work brings that legitimacy, to which it owes its existence, to light, reflective judgement can only refer, then, to one specific object: 'In fact,

---

9 Kant, *Critique of Judgement*, §40, p. 102.
10 Kant, *Critique of Judgement*, §29, p. 78.

the judgement of Taste always takes the form of a singular judgement about an Object'.[11] In a pure definition of aesthetic purposiveness, reflective aesthetic lays a claim to autonomy.[12] Applying other kinds of judgement to the work, such as moral judgement, would be heteronomous, and in the sense that 'we shall have an Understanding judging sensibly or a sense representing its objects by means of concepts',[13] would be a contradiction in itself.

At the same time, it is clear that disinterested pleasure does not constitute the end of appreciation of the beautiful but, rather, a necessary precondition, its very starting point.[14] For it is the appreciation of the beautiful that gives rise to an interest in the existence of the observed object, an interest in enjoying its beauty.[15] There is no reason why pleasure should not give rise to interest, whereby the observer comes to be interested in the continued existence of the object of [her] perception. The interest that the observer may experience, the pleasure in 'aesthetic ideas' is an animal pleasure, is bodily and sensual and can be linked to value judgements of moral ideas [which, according to Kant, do not constitute pleasure].[16] If it is the reflective judgements about the aesthetic object, which produce a *sensus communis*, and that must be applied to all of human rationality, then it is the 'feelings of respect for moral ideas'[17]

---

11 Kant, *Critique of Judgement*, §33, p. 94.

12 Kant, *Critique of Judgement*, §32, pp. 91–3.

13 Kant, *Critique of Judgement*, §15, p. 48.

14 See Kant, *Critique of Judgement*, §23, p. 75: 'Moreover, the former delight is very different from the latter in kind. For the beautiful is directly attended with a feeling of the furtherance of life, and is thus compatible with charms and a playful imagination.'

15 Kant, *Critique of Judgement*, §41, p. 104.

16 Kant, *Critique of Judgement*, §54, p. 131–6.

that give rise to a self-esteem as 'an esteem for humanity within us'.[18] In her regard for moral ideas, the human being finds herself to be a member of all humanity. She finds in herself what she considers to be worthy of recognition in others, and thus begins to find regard for herself.

In reflective judgement applied to the work of art, the judging subject ascertains her belonging to humanity, comparing its standards of values to her own. Ascribing value to aesthetic judgement and the experience of beauty are possible when experiencing pleasure through beauty makes way for the feeling of 'intensification of the feeling of being alive'. However, to look for the beautiful because one dares to pin hope on it with the assumption that it contributes to the sharpening of an 'animal' interest only belongs in the realm of barbarism. Judgement would then be clouded because, even before such judgement is possible, the perception of beauty would be obfuscated by a kind of charm and the stirring of emotions, or worse, an erotic interest.[19]

No interest can therefore underlie the observation of the beautiful. At the same time, the beautiful is a symbol of the moral and the good.[20] For Kant, symbols are analogies in the form of indirect representation. While beauty has an immediate appeal, it derives its claim to validation of all else only by way of reflection. Taste does not shut itself off in the self-satisfaction of subjective perception; rather, it steps out into the intelligible, of which it is a part. Reflective judgement produces the innate

---

17 Kant, *Critique of Judgement*, p. 163.

18 Kant, *Critique of Judgement*, p. 163.

19 Kant, *Critique of Judgement*, §44, pp. 134–5. For a similar Pygmalionesque aberration, see Felix Liebrecht, *Zur Volkskunde* (Heilbronn: Henninger, 1879), p. 138f.

20 Kant, *Critique of Judgement*, §59, p. 180.

possibility that the subject may correspond with an extraneous nature in consonance, as the unity of practical and theoretical faculties, in a shared and common but hitherto-unknown fashion.[21] The sequential succession of disinterest and interest is also to be found where the beautiful is connected with the morally good. The morally good is 'necessarily bound up with an interest—not with one of the kind that are antecedent to the judgement upon the delight, but, rather, with one that judgement itself for the first time calls into existence'.[22]

The beauty of nature, which is conducive to the moral uplift of humankind, may be allowed to evoke human interest,[23] because that which is naturally beautiful does not depend on the exclusive consonance of the diverse, the self-determination of its purpose; experiencing the naturally beautiful with interest does not disrupt either the object or the validity of judgement, since it does not contain within it the principal of autonomy.[24]

---

21 Kant, *Critique of Judgement*, p. 181.

22 Kant, *Critique of Judgement*, p. 181.

23 Kant, *Critique of Judgement*, §42, p. 128: 'But, on the other hand, I do maintain that to take an *immediate interest* in the beauty of *nature* (not merely to have taste in judging it) is always a mark of a good soul; and that, where this interest is habitual, it is at least indicative of a temper of mind favourable to the moral feeling that it should readily associate itself with the *contemplation of nature*' (emphasis as in original).

24 Kant, *Critique of Judgement*, §48, p. 141.

Kant II: *Disinterestedness and* sensus communis

According to Kant, there is no necessary connection between the work of art and any given idea of the good. The beautiful cannot be adjudged according to moral standards because it is governed entirely by formal purposiveness. However, beauty can be seen as a symbol, as an indirect representation of the good insofar as both the discourses—the aesthetic and the moral—seek to bring judgement to bear upon 'everyone else'. There is a kind of reason that governs aesthetic judgement, which, though differentiated from the theoretical, is far from the solipsism of the solely subjective assertion of the qualities of a work of art, which is resistant to any kind of reasoning. Judgement of the artefact occurs in the processes of doubt and assurance. It is not so much the agreement with what is known or the assertion of correspondence with all else but, rather, the inability of this tentative, doubting judgement to be firmly founded that constitutes common sense.

In other words, it is the very autonomy of the work of art and the morally indifferent attitude of the disinterested observer that imply a certain morality which is a result of the inevitable uncertainty of aesthetic judgement and the permanence of doubt. And because the individual subject cannot be entirely certain about her own judgement, she must assume the consensus of all humanity. It is in discovery of her subjective generality and the generality of separation that the subject encounters herself as belonging to all of humanity. It is not semantic substantialities that produce the *sensus communis* but, rather, the general nature of doubt, the boundlessness of the reflective process, the uncertain nature of judgement.

What is it about the moment of disinterestedness, the construct of a human being without drive or sensuality, that demands a solution and expression? How does one imagine a subjectivity that is free of all particularities? What is a subjectivity that does not distinguish itself from other subjectivities, given that it is free from its own specific forms and modalities of individual being, its 'being-itself'? Which is the subject that judges the individual object?

The disinterested subject is the subject only in the moment that she suspends herself in observing an object that demands nothing of her. There is no other interest than this disinterested pleasure. There are no expectations of her; she operates in a state of freedom, that of freedom from herself, from her own interests, drives, struggles, preferences and compulsions. It is the freedom of a subject who is free of herself. In realizing the freedom to which she owes her existence, and in understanding the compulsions that the work had to overcome in order to realize this freedom and its autonomy, and that are still visible as veins and warts, the subject achieves the constitution of herself as free. In the process of realizing this autonomy, the handing over of the subject to the heteronomy of the work of art is rendered complete. She surrenders to that which stands before her.

In this sense, at the heart of this constellation, that of an autonomous work and the work as heteronomous to the subject, lies a disparity, a struggle between the constitution of an autonomy on the one hand, and the necessity to suspend this autonomy in favour of a pure and complete understanding of the other, given that it is indeed autonomous, of what is fundamentally alien. It appears, then, that autonomy seems to suggest the authority of the autonomous as heteronomous.

Yet, the autonomy of the work of art is neither dominant nor does it ask for subservience. The work of art is confronted not by a purely passive subject reduced entirely to its receptive capacity but, rather, by a subject that strives to understand the freedom of that which is different from itself. Rilke's exhortation, 'you must change your life', is less an appeal by the stone than it is the conclusion that the subject, which has become aware of herself through the work of art, draws with reference to herself. In the end, in order to articulate as well as to hear this call for transformation, a comparison between itself and the fragmented sculpture becomes necessary. The stone does not demand anything, not even that the offer of freedom made by the autonomous work of art be accepted. The Apollo of antiquity, as he stands before the observer in Rilke's poem, robbed of his head, his arms, his sex, his legs, in his unintendedness, in complete absence of the intention to have been imagined in his present form, represents the purposelessness or remoteness of purpose of the work of art: it can become a paradigm for freedom due to the fact that it was not created in order to be what it has become. The demand made by every metaphysics of art—that the work be overpowering—stands in opposition to freedom, and freedom is paradigmatically articulated within the work of art which follows no purpose other than to realize itself in its autonomy. The Rilkean observer witnesses this in the surviving fragment of Apollo—an articulation of perfection that is nevertheless communicated by the fragmented body.

❄

KANT II

Moreover, the subject does not stop at the silent perception of the object, it does not dwell in a wordless reception. Rather, it transforms the process of perception into the process of reflection. Sensuality is transformed into language, the apparently immediate given is transformed into the mediated, pure perception is followed by reflection by the subject on what is perceived and on perception as performed through language. This reflects the communicability of perception, of desire.[1] There are two ways in which the immediately given is not overshadowed, sensuality is not disavowed but preserved through the modality of reflection: as reflection about the object; and as reflection of the subject about itself and the modalities of its own responses to the object. The subject places before all of human reason the mediated, that which is separated from the immediately given, but upholds immediacy in reflection, and thereby exposes it to a process of comparison within which the validity of one's own reflection abides as a disposition. As a consequence of the subjective generality of her reflective judgement, in the process of comparison, the subject is constituted as a universal subject. The disinterestedness of the subject vouches for the possibility that it recreates herself as free through mediation with the aesthetic object, which demonstrates, indicates, reveals, the possibility of freedom, holding it as the very monstrance of freedom before her own eyes. The subject led by interest, however, is one which constantly finds, replicates, duplicates and tautologically reproduces herself, reaffirms her identity in the constancy of her self through endless reproduction as the same. It finds what it

---

1 Kant, *Critique of Judgement*, §44, p. 135: 'The universal communicability of a pleasure involves in its very concept that the pleasure is not one of enjoyment arising out of mere sensation, but must be one of reflection. Hence aesthetic art, as art which is beautiful, is one having for its standard the reflective judgement and not bodily sensation.'

expects to find in the heteronomous, and disputes the very existence of the heteronomous in its autonomy. It constructs identity as an agreement with that which was always present as such and such, has existed always as it was, for which the heteronomous is supposed to supply proof.

The disinterested subject represents a rupture in the totality or the continuity of the social. She ceases to be a person.[2] In the weave of the social as a fabric of particular interests and as exchange of opinions by everyone with everyone, the disinterestedness of the aesthetic subject represents a gap, a break, a void, or flaw. Its quality is defined through communication with that which faces the aesthetic object, and not through participation in the exchange of opinions and points of view that constitute the social fabric. The disinterested aesthetic subject decides in favour of non-participation. The decision is far less a refusal than it is an attempt at a different form of communication, that of non-agreement, of friction and tension. Foregoing the possibility of interestedness, relinquishing the opportunity to be understood as a complete subject, renouncing the abundance that has been supplanted by growing separation, turns the aesthetic subject into an asocial subject. She situates herself outside the conflict between particular interests and the rapprochement resulting from this conflict, outside particular interests and the problem of their conciliation, keeping society in a state of unrest, thereby insisting on incommensurability.

Disinterested pleasure, however, does indeed give rise to an interestedness in the continued existence of the aesthetic object, the work of art, a desire that seeks to protect itself and in which

---

2 Person in the sense of Luhmann. See Niklas Luhmann, *Die Form* 'Person' in *Soziologische Aufklärung*, VOL. 6: *Die Soziologie und der Mensch* (Wiesbaden: VS Verlag für Sozialwissenschaften, 2005), p. 146: 'Persons serve as the structural linking of psychic and social systems.'

the subject enjoys herself and her relationship with the world. Through this desire, the subject discovers that she agrees with the world and is at home in it, and that her perception is not mere fiction, that it is neither confusion nor error but, rather, a correspondence, an equivocation of the perceived and inhabited world.[3]

The desire of the subject for the experience of consonance with the world is impossible to eradicate, and it leaves a mark on reflective judgement. As much as judgement is reflection on the object of perception, it is still a reflection upon the mode of perception and its consequence, which is pleasure. To the categorical certainty that aesthetic judgement cannot be a defining one is the added difficulty that it cannot be a pure judgement either. As a result, it is a judgement in which the sensual, the 'animal' (according to Kant), continues to exist, and must dialectically reveal itself to that which must be given consideration as it separates itself from reason.

As a result, reflective judgement proves to be problematic not only because it cannot be a cognitive judgement but because it also admixes the sensual in the judgement of beauty. Reflective judgement is judgement that, in repeatedly affirming itself, undermines its own validity. The process of judgement does not begin with perception and does not end with judgement but, rather, evolves into an evaluation of judgement and its consequences and implications, its own inconsistence and instability. It does so in the process that cannot be concluded even if it does come to an end given the limits of time. This turns the reflective

---

3 Immanuel Kant, *Reflexion*, 1820a, *Akademie-Ausgabe*, VOL. XVI (Berlin: Georg Reimer, 1900), p. 127: 'Die schönen Dinge zeigen an, daß der Mensch in die Welt passe und selbst eine Anschauung mit den Gesetzen seiner Anschauung stimme' ('Beautiful things indicate that man fits into the world and that his worldview is in concordance with the laws of his worldview').

judgement into a judgement about and against itself. That is why it does not suffice to argue that the work of art sets off a process of reflection as long as one is unwilling to subject oneself to the assertion of negativity of reflection and its subversive consequences.

How can *sensus communis*, as discussed by Kant, rest on reflective judgement which has no end and has no means to defend itself against its own destructive potential? As judgement incapable of being a defining judgement, it arrives at no conclusions, it cannot exclude anything, whether the definite or the defining. As frenzy of reason beset by sensuality that knows no limits, it is subject to the disintegrative process of diremption. How, then, should reflective judgement, which places itself vertically in the rupture, reconcile itself with the horizontality of the social, with the fabric that, while it is being woven, is interrupted by judgement?

It all comes down to what Kant characterizes as the category of 'Rücksichtnahme', or respect (see *Critique of Judgement*, §40, p. 123). Communal sense is both collective reason and a sense of the collective and communal. This respect is the consideration for the judgement by others, which is supposed to become a part of reflection as an expression of the sense for the collective that is constituted through this respect. This consideration for the opinions of others is a corrective, for private opinions which like to be taken as objective. It is in this exercise of respect that collective and communal reason is forged, where reflective judgement as subjective is in consonance with the judgement of others, and its frenzy comes to rest. It is this 'broadened thought'[4] that requires of the subject

---

4 Kant, *Critique of Judgement*, §40, p. 124: 'While the following maxims of common human understanding do not properly come in here as constituent parts of the critique of taste, they may still serve to elucidate its

that she subjects herself to comparison, and tests the consonance of her own thinking with that of others. The respect for the judgement of others corrects the judgement of the subject and propels the widening of the subjective into the collective.

The subject expects from herself a consideration for the judgement of others, to ensure their right to consideration for their judgement. This right to consideration is the right of those who do not participate.[5] Yet it is also the right that those who do not participate make available to others. Not because the balancing of particular interests requires consideration, but because reason and insight require it, the non-participant as the sovereign of this right concedes this right to others. In this non-participation, in the act and through the offering of one-sided and unconditional respect, the disinterested subject institutes the right to an antithetical politics, within which community constitutes itself as society.

---

fundamental propositions. They are these: (1) to think for oneself; (2) to think from the standpoint of everyone else; (3) always to think consistently. The first is the maxim of *unprejudiced* thought, the second that of *broadened* thought, the third that of *consistent* thought.'

5 Christoph Menke, *Kritik der Rechte* (Berlin: Suhrkamp Verlag, 2015), p. 354.

The Sublime: *Kant and Schiller*

In contrast to the category of beauty is the category of the sublime. Kant locates the sublime as sensation in the mind of the human being; it only comes to play a role when the human being is able to overcome not only her outer but also her inner nature. However, nature only gives cause for imagining the sublime. 'Sublimity, therefore, does not reside in any of the things of nature, but only in our own mind, insofar as we may become conscious of our own superiority over nature within, and thus also over nature outside us (as exerting influence upon us).'[1]

The beautiful and the sublime relate to different ways of interacting with the world.[2]

> The *beautiful* is what pleases in the mere judging of it [. . .]. From this it follows at once that it must please apart from all interest. The *sublime* is what pleases immediately through its resistance to the interest of the

---

1 Kant, *Critique of Judgement*, §28, p. 94.

2 For the relationship between the sublime and the beautiful, see Carsten Zelle, 'Schönheit und Erhabenheit. Der Anfang doppelter Ästhetik bei Boileau, Dennis, Bodmer und Breitinger' in Christine Pries (ed.), *Das Erhabene. Zwischen Grenzerfahrung und Größenwahn* (Weinheim: Acta Humanora, 1989), pp. 55–75.

senses. [. . .] The beautiful prepares us to love something, even nature, apart from any interest: the sublime to esteem something highly even in opposition to our (sensuous) interest.[3]

Beauty is a way of practising love. Love has little to do with interest in the object—it occurs solely on account of the beauty of the object of love. In its beauty, the world becomes an object of the kind of love which, while not led by interest, justifies the human being's impression of being capable of resonating with it.

There is a correspondence between the human being's ability to perceive and the appearance of the world in her perception. Beauty reveals to the human being that her perceptions are valid. The world opens up and shows the observing subject not only the fact that nature corresponds with her intention directed at knowing,[4] but also that she is welcome in the entirety of her existence.

Conversely, the feeling of the sublime as 'negative interest'[5] is associated with the suggestion of fear and teaches the human being the quality of reverence, not that of love. Reverence also extends to objects that may be directly antithetical to the interests of the human being. The sublime teaches humankind the art of transcending herself as a way of overcoming her own sensual interests, given that moral principles require that particular facts continue being given consideration, even when such consideration endangers one's own integrity. The sublime encourages the setting aside of subjective interests, where outer as well as inner nature is overcome, and it teaches the human being 'to feel the sublimity of [her] own vocation even over

---

3 Kant, *Critique of Judgement*, §29, p. 97.

4 Introduction to Kant, *Critique of Judgement*, pp. 30–1.

5 Kant, *Critique of Judgement*, §23, p. 76

nature'.[6] While beauty teaches love, the sublime teaches defer-ence and steers the human being towards her purpose, namely, that of transcending nature in the external world and herself as nature. The sublime implies morality.

Whereas beauty is encountered both in the field of art and in observing nature, in its various effects on the mind, the sublime is only to be experienced in observing nature. The work of art cannot communicate the suggestion of fear which is an inevitable part of experiencing the sublime. The relation between beauty and morality is symbolic and indirectly representational, while the sublime, even when mediated, appeals to the human being's sense of purpose to rise above her own boundedness, and to tran-scend her inherent nature. In that respect, both beauty and the sublime imply freedom: beauty as an end in itself, in that it has no obligations with regard to any sphere that is not identical to itself; and the sublime as a reminder of the human being's innate potential to be more than she already is.

In his writings on aesthetic education,[7] the Kallias letters[8] and in the writing on the sublime,[9] Schiller sharpens the differ-entiation between beauty and the sublime. 'The beautiful is merely well deserved of *man* [. . .]'.[10] 'Through beauty alone

---

6 Kant, *Critique of Judgement*, §28, p. 92.

7 Friedrich Schiller, 'Ueber die ästhetische Erziehung des Menschen in einer Reihe von Briefen' (1795) in Lieselotte Blumenthal, Benno von Wiese (eds), *Schillers Werke: Nationalausgabe*, VOL. 20 (Weimar: Herman Böhlaus Nach-folger, 1962), pp. 309–412.

8 Friedrich Schiller, letters to Körner dated 25 January, 25 February, and 1 March 1793. In *Werke*, VOL. 26 (Weimar: Herman Böhlaus Nachfolger, 1992), pp. 174–6, 219–28.

9 Friedrich Schiller, 'Über das Erhabene' (1801) in *Werke*, VOL. 21 (Weimar: Herman Böhlaus Nachfolger, 1963), pp. 38–56.

10 Schiller, 'Über das Erhabene' p. 52.

would we therefore eternally never learn, that we are determined and able to prove ourselves as pure intelligences'[11] Through the not-beautiful, the sublime, the human being is elevated to her real purpose.[12] This sublimity is the sublimity of the heroic, which 'face to face with evil fate'[13] dares to march towards her purpose: freedom.

While Schiller believes that beauty mediates between nature and reason in the human being, he allocates to the sublime a particular function which beauty cannot fulfil: to remind the human being of her dignity.[14] Beauty has a softening effect, and only the sublime can remind the human being of her eternal destiny and her real homeland.[15] However, as long as art blends beauty with the sublime,[16] it is able to uplift the human being to a true citizen of nature and the world.[17]

At the same time, Schiller agrees with Plato's view of art in general (*Politeia*, 595a), namely, that it is deceptive and illusory.

---

11 Schiller, 'Über das Erhabene', p. 43.

12 Schiller, 'Über das Erhabene', p. 43.

13 Schiller, 'Über das Erhabene', p. 52.

14 Schiller, 'Über das Erhabene', p. 53.

15 Schiller, 'Über das Erhabene', p. 53.

16 Schiller, 'Über das Erhabene', p. 53: 'The capacity of the sublime is one of the noblest aptitudes of man. Beauty is useful, but does not go beyond man. The sublime applies to the pure spirit. The sublime must be joined to the beautiful to complete the aesthetic education, and to enlarge man's heart beyond the sensuous world. Without the beautiful there would be an eternal strife between our natural and rational destiny. If we only thought of our vocation as spirits we should be strangers to this sphere of life. Without the sublime, beauty would make us forget our dignity. Enervated wedded to this transient state, we should lose sight of our true country. We are only perfect citizens of nature when the sublime is wedded to the beautiful.' Cited from Friedrich Schiller, *Aesthetical and Philosophical Essays* (2013).

17 Schiller, 'Über das Erhabene', p. 43.

In characterizing beauty as being of service to humanity, he locates it in the sensual—beauty entraps the human being whereas the sublime shows them an escape.[18]

Since beauty only serves human interest, is it insufficient in times when the human species as a tragic species wants to transcend itself towards its destiny. Beauty is for a prosperous race. But a tragic race, one needs to try to touch with the sublime.[19]

For Kant, the autonomy of art is based on the unfoundability of aesthetic judgement, on the impossibility of arriving at cognitive judgement from aesthetic judgement, and at a defining judgement from reflective judgement. The reflexive movement of judgement, based on doubt, gives rise to a community which connects the judging subject with all other subjects. In the shift from sensual experience to reflection, in linguistic comparison and in the practice of consideration lies the possibility of building a collective consciousness. This is manifest in the 'communicability of pleasure' as well as in transcending the limits of subjectivity, of private opinion, towards an intersubjective universal. Beauty and morality, respect and consideration for moral ideas, are freely occurring comparisons, parallelizations, crossfadings, which neither compel nor presuppose each other; nevertheless, each sheds light on the other. The sphere of morality and the sphere of beauty are logically separate, and if they communicate, they do so indirectly, through symbols, analogies, in the form of indirect representation. There is no obligation to assess beauty in terms of its relevance to the sphere of the social, its worth for that which is outside of the beautiful. Even in this respect, beauty remains autonomous.

---

18 Schiller, 'Über das Erhabene', p. 45.

19 Friedrich Schiller, Letter to Süvern, dated 26 July 1800. In *Werke*, VOL. 30, *Briefwechsel 1.11.1798–31.12.1800* (Weimar: Herman Böhlaus Nachfolger, 1961), p. 177.

❋

THE SUBLIME

Schiller, on the other hand, declares beauty to be a legislating principle: 'To give freedom through freedom is a fundamental law of this realm'[20] Art is praised as a site of freedom, and beauty as freedom in appearance.[21] For Schiller, autonomy is undercut precisely by this affirmation, in which beauty becomes a model for freedom which should, beyond art, in life, become reality. The description of beauty as freedom in appearance is tied to a caveat, a doubt about its value. Since beauty as manifest in sensory experience is inferior to the sublime, it shackles humankind to her nature, and obstructs her rise to her true purpose. As deceptive appearance, beauty places itself above and before the true purpose of the human being. The comfort that, in Kant's view, beautiful things afford the human being—so that she can belong in the world—becomes in the case of Schiller an argument against beauty. It is a false comfort, offered contrary to insight and reason, a mere palliative. Thus, through praise of beauty as the realm of freedom, Schiller in fact disavows beauty. He only allows it as long as it represents the law in the sphere of appearance, which should fulfil itself where the struggle of humankind as a tragic species for freedom unfolds.

Compared to Kant, we can see the shift in the social location of beauty in Schiller's writings. In Schiller's work, beauty is expected to show its achievements with respect to the social sphere, to prove its worth in relation to something greater and more meaningful: human destiny. In the face of this task, beauty falls short; it does not possess the rigour of the sublime so required by the human being who perceives herself as tragic. As solely of service to the human being, it is sufficient for the

---

20 Schiller, letter to Süvern, 26 July 1800.

21 Friedrich Schiller, 'Aus den ästhetischen Vorlesungen' in *Werke*, VOL. 21, p. 83.

human being, while the human being doesn't suffice for herself any more. She must grow beyond herself into the realm of 'pure spirit', to the laws of which she is supposed to mould. Beauty is judged by its effect, as weakening and softening, and art divides itself into that which embellishes the present into a kind of art that in its appearance seeks to call forth the effect of the sublime. There is thus the new possibility in art, that of the not-beautiful, which, while it induces little pleasure, equips the human being to break free of the shackles of an incidental existence.

Art that combines elements of beauty and sublimity serves a hitherto-unknown purpose: it shows the human being that in the sphere of the aesthetic, she can be a part of nature, without, on the one hand, serving as its slave, and on the other, of having to lose her claim to the realm of the intelligible, of knowledge and reason.

An easy shift in the value of beauty whereby its comforting, harmonizing function is marked by a negative index, requires that it is complemented by the sublime in order to counter-balance this newly arisen flaw. For Kant, the sublime may be found in nature, but not in art; for Schiller, it serves as a necessary corrective to merely beautiful art in order that it yields more than just a demonstration of comfort for the lackadaisical citizen.

Beauty is thus only one of the many possibilities of art, and its value can be measured according to which role it is able to play in consonance with the sublime when it comes to human purpose. Schiller introduces a third category that mediates between sensuality and knowledge, between beauty and the sublime, namely, that of play,[22] which in the sphere of appearance

---

22 Schiller, *Ästhetische Erziehung*, p. 410. 'In the midst of the awful realm of powers, and of the sacred realm of laws, the aesthetic creative impulse is

seeks to unite the powers of the terrifying empire and the laws of the 'holy realm'. It is in play that the appearance of the sublime prepares the human being for her purpose, just as the appearance of beauty gives her pleasure. Appearance beyond appearance of the beautiful is able to create truth-effects, spurred on by the drive towards an aesthetic education, which is directed not only at art but also at the greater realm of play which encompasses the realm of art. The aesthetic as the sphere of the sensual, which includes both natural beauty and beauty in art, but is not limited to either, acts as the formative force in the formation of social reality.

Along with the drive towards form, sense and play, there is the formative drive; it precedes the play drive which is related to the aesthetic nature of all appearances,[23] and helps to create the world in which it has its own place. What is the object of the aesthetic formative drive, when the social being and her transformation is the object of the sense drive, existence and identity are the objects of the form drive, and the living form beyond time is the object of the play drive (in Schiller's perspective, they all have beauty as their object)?[24] The object of the formative drive is the human being as the bearer of these drives, who should come to enjoy the freedom that the joyful realm of play promises, wherein the human being works on forming herself and in so doing also contributes to the formation of the

---

building unawares a third joyous realm of play and of appearance, in which it releases mankind from all the shackles of circumstance and frees him from everything that may be called constraint, whether physical or moral'—from Friedrich Schiller, *On the Aesthetic Education of Man* (Reginald Snell trans.) (New York: Dover Publications, 2004), p. 242.

23 Schiller *Ästhetische Erziehung*, p. 58.

24 See Alexander García Düttman, 'Leben und Schönheit' in Düttmann, *Was weiß Kunst?* (Konstanz: Konstanz University Press, 2015), p. 104.

social body. This process of shaping occurs between the two poles of beauty and the sublime, in the sphere of the aesthetic, which is both illusory and real, given that the human being who becomes the object of the formative drive operates out of the medium of appearances into that of reality. In the aesthetic formative drive, the human being mediates sense and form drive. She works on the form of the social body in introducing the moment of self-formation through her identity, treats identity as malleable matter, and, with the help of her self, uses her own changeability as a medium of social formation, and herself as the agent and instrument of social change.

Compared with Kant, positions have shifted in Schiller's hierarchy. The formative drive deploys beauty and the sublime as means to forge a community, but beauty does not lead by way of reflective judgement to the formation of a sense of community. For Schiller, both beauty and the sublime have a purpose and a value which can be measured against the scale of their contribution to the 'joyous realm', where all shackles are broken. Situated within an economy of values, the value of beauty is based on whether or not it is able to realize its own fundamental principle of granting freedom through freedom. The freedom of beauty encounters its own limits in this demarcation. The value of autonomy lies in the heteronomous, its social being. Its value is the value which it possesses for an other.[25]

---

25 On the concept of value, see Thomas Hobbes, *Leviathan of The Matter, Forme and Power of a Commonwealth, Ecclesiastical and Civil* (Cambridge: Cambridge University Press, 1996), p. 63. 'The *Value*, or WORTH of a man, is as of all other things, his Price; that is to say, so much as would be given for the use of his Power: and therefore is not absolute; but a thing dependant on the need and judgement of another.'

While Kant's view of autonomy of the aesthetic, reflective judgement is a result of the flaw that it cannot be accorded any kind of objective necessity, for Schiller, autonomy is a pedagogical resource. It now has the purpose of education. What happens in the field of art can be seen as a model for a fruitful social and political freedom. It only needs a small change, a slight shift in its objective, and it is only a matter of who is posing the question regarding the value of autonomy, and who answers it, for it to have an exemplary influence on freedom. This is because the duty to have an effect transforms art; irrespective of the meaning given to freedom and what it is expected to yield, that it should at all be subject to laws gives rise to a contradiction in the discourse on freedom. This contradiction can only be resolved when a particular instance is granted the right or assumes for itself the right to define the socially tolerable extent of freedom, and, with it, the extent to which art makes use of that freedom. The obligation to grant freedom invalidates the very idea of freedom. The pedagogical instrumentalization that all the totalitarian systems since Schiller have been responsible for becomes clear in this fundamental principle. These fundamental laws, irrespective of who articulates them, require art to serve society. It may be allowed to keep its freedom, as long as it performs the task given to it of reminding the human being of her purpose. What could be thought of as the purpose of humankind has changed constantly since the Enlightenment. Without going into greater detail, it suffices to say that there have been and continue to be totalitarian systems which prefer to dictate to the individual, the civic national subject, her purpose, and forbid others from having the same purpose, deny them the right to be identifiable as individuals, invisibilized and annihilated them. It needs to be pointed out that in Schiller, one finds a concept of art that is suited to being a pedagogical means towards the education of humankind, where its freedom and its autonomy is justified precisely because it is a means to an end. That it is at all given a function—the freedom to give freedom—indicates that for Schiller, this freedom, which refers to nothing other than itself and follows no purpose, had become suspect. The autonomy of the aesthetic requires justification, and it finds justification through morality. The scandal of a human sphere that is not bound by or to anything other than itself is done away with by calling upon the fundamental principle of freedom. While in Kant there seems to be no relation between beauty and the good, except on the convoluted paths of indirect symbolization, there is the attempt to build bridges whereby, by means of the moral, the aesthetic is attached to the social. The question whether the aesthetic satisfies the law is a question pertaining to the moral value of the aesthetic, which, should it not satisfy this law, proves itself to be useless, senseless, purposeless. The inherent contradiction in this law condemns the aesthetic to failure. It cannot resolve the contradiction between freedom and subservience to a law that is expected to determine freedom. Thus, just as beauty was considered to be inferior to the sublime, so is henceforth the aesthetic considered to be inferior to the moral.

Stendhal and the Promise of Happiness

Schiller rejects the idea that beauty promises happiness as suggested by Kant.[1] According to Kant, in both types of judgement—judgement on beauty as well as judgement on the morally good—the subject experiences the exhilarating correspondence of her judgement, free of all obligations, based on freedom and invoking it, with the objects of judgement and with humankind, with whom she agrees on a world shared through reflection.

Stendhal reintroduces the happiness motif in the larger context of a treatise on love. He says, 'La beauté n'est que la promesse de bonheur'.[2] However, the promise of happiness is in itself a problematic one, because this statement can be read in two ways. Beauty is either exclusively and nothing other than a promise of happiness, or, beauty is 'nothing, but' or only a promise of happiness.[3]

---

1 Kant, *Critique of Judgement*, §41, p. 218 as well as in the passage from 1771 quoted earlier, in which he argues that beauty shows the human being that she is a part of the world.

2 Stendhal, *De L'Amour* (1857) (Paris: Edition établie et commentée par Henri Martineau, 1957), p. 39.

3 See Christoph Menke, 'Die Schönheit zwischen Anschauung and Rausch' (2011), in Menke, *Die Kraft der Kunst*, p. 41 ff.

In both ways of reading, formal criteria for defining beauty are excluded. Beauty is not to be found in formal autonomy or in autonomous freedom from purpose but, rather, in its function with respect to the happiness of the human being. In the first reading, this is the only function: that which cannot promise happiness cannot be beautiful. Only that which fulfils the function of providing happiness can be considered beautiful. All other functions of beauty are irrelevant. It is about the effects of beauty beyond social frameworks within which beauty can be enlisted to meet all kinds of ends, whether that of building social capital, of teaching and instruction, of self-representation, or the representation of power, among others. The idea of beauty as the promise of happiness is aimed at the timeless and trans-social human core. Irrespective of how beauty is constituted, regardless of how it may have felt, observed, heard, tasted or smelt, it continues to have the same function.

The second reading (that beauty is only a promise) greatly weakens the relevance of the function of beauty: beauty is only the promise of happiness, and promises may be fulfilled or they may not. What is merely a promise in the mind of the one that makes the promise, is a promise without intention to fulfil it, a false promise, and, a false promise is the same as a lie.

In Stendhal's definition, we again see the two faces of beauty, one of which Schiller had tried to get rid of in favour of the sublime: beauty exists solely at the service of the human being, as a substitute for real social transformation, a mere palliative. Beauty represents the happiness that, in unhappy times, takes on the character of a lie. The tragic historical circumstances in which Schiller found himself demanded not the search for happiness but the struggle for dignity. To conceive of beauty as the promise of happiness is nothing but the return of the deceptiveness of the appearance of beauty.

❋

At the same time, the 'only' may refer to the position of beauty in an economy of values within which it assumes a subordinate position. If beauty is only a promise, it is also a promise among many others, and while revolutions, for instance, promise equality and freedom, beauty only promises happiness. The *'n'est que*—nothing, but, only—is the crucial link. It determines whether beauty and happiness are seen as mere trifles in society as a whole, as being of relatively little significance when compared with truth, purpose, emancipation, freedom, justice, etc., or whether the *'n'est que*—'nothing but'—claims to be a more precise determination of the function of beauty: as little more than a promise of happiness.

Even in the case of the latter reading, Stendhal builds a constantly self-generating deferment into the definition of beauty. It does not matter whether it is nothing but or only the promise of happiness. Beauty remains a promise that knows neither fulfilment nor disappointment; it always lingers in its function of referencing happiness. It is in this characteristic that beauty acquires the quality of looking beyond itself. It is never quite temporal, and appears to always go beyond and towards something that lies in the future. It seems to be in appearance, and as such fades into the present of the human being, whose happiness is always only of the remembered kind, for there is no happiness in the present moment without the residue of earlier and of the earliest-ever happiness. In the promise of beauty in the present, the past of the subject experiencing happiness is tied to the possibility of happiness in the future.

On the other hand, beauty remains an eternal promisor, a promise of an eternally deferred future, which will never materialize in the present. The happiness which beauty claims to know something about is located in a permanence of unattainability, where it both beckons and evades, at the same time as

❋

its communication is mediated through its own existence, and it is in this mediacy as something promised that it reveals itself as unattainable.

Beauty as a promise of happiness (and nothing but) is in that sense comforting to the human being, giving her a sense that she belongs in the world, and the string of lies that binds her like Tantalus to pleasures of this world, without offering the hope that the world can be a source of enjoyment and that happiness could be attained through this enjoyment. The present of happiness is that of the unattainable, the present of an evasive future.

Nietzsche I

The connection made by Stendhal between beauty and happiness becomes central in Nietzsche. In *On the Genealogy of Morality*, he refers to Stendhal as follows:

> As I said, Stendhal, no less a sensualist than Schopenhauer but with a more happily adjusted personality, emphasises another effect of beauty: 'beauty promises happiness', to him, the fact of the matter is precisely the excitement of the will ('of interest') through beauty.'[1]

And there is no doubt that this reference to the writer is tied to a categorical turn away from Kant: 'Since Kant, the expression 'without interest' has turned all ideas of art, beauty, knowledge, wisdom into trite pablum.[2]

Nietzsche does come back to Stendhal. Yet, in his reprise, he does away with the Janus face of promise, namely, that a promise can be broken and that its fulfilment in the future is

---

1 Friedrich Nietzsche, *On the Genealogy of Morality* (Keith Anselm-Pearson ed., Carol Diethe trans.) (Cambridge: Cambridge University Press, 2007), p. 75. Also see Friedrich Nietzsche, *Zur Genealogie der Moral, Kritische Studienausgabe*, VOL. 5 (Giorgio Colli and Mazzino Montinari eds) (Munich: Deutscher Taschenbuch Verlag, 1988), p. 348 f.

2 Nietzsche, *Zur Genealogie der Moral*, VOL. 10, p. 243.

an eternal deferment beyond any kind of present. In Nietzsche, the relationship between beauty and happiness is free of all ambivalence.

Beauty that awakens interest has its effect in the moment, directly, and physically.

> All art acts as suggestion to all the muscles and senses that have been active in the case of the naïve artistic human being: […] it speaks to this kind of fine excitability of the body. […] All art works as a tonic, enhances power, fires desire (that is, the feeling of power), spurs finer memories of inebriety—there is an innate recollection that appears in such circumstances: this is the fleeting return of a distant and transient world of sensations.[3]

Nietzsche not only does away with reflection, which in Kant ennobled simple sense perception and animal lust, but also the tension that is a result of the character of the promise in Stendhal. Given that beauty has a direct impact on the body, the promise of beauty is fulfilled in the moment in which it is experienced. At the same time, the memory of a past happiness is awakened in the subject in experiencing beauty; in happiness, the past and the present become one. The exhilaration caused by art—accompanied by the enervation of the muscles, growing resilience and the return of a distant and fleeting world of sensations—is the exhilaration experienced by a subject within whom are active those original forces, that is, in a primordial sense, in a manner in which they connect with the origins of art and the origins of humankind. It is through art that the distance between her present and the origins of her creativity can be

---

3 Nietzsche, *Zur Genealogie der Moral*, VOL. 13, p. 296.

bridged; for her, art is the medium through which to reach out across epochs and time.

In the very moment when it is perceived, beauty has the effect of strengthening the physical constitution of the human being:

> It is the relationship between the concept of art and life that is of essence (here): both psychologically as well as physiologically, it can be seen as the greatest stimulant, as that which eternally/always pushes towards life, towards eternal life.[4]

Ugliness is measured no more against formal criteria than beauty; ugly is that which diminishes vitality. It is not a part of art, it is its antithesis:

> Ugliness, that which is contradictory to art, that which is excluded by art, its negation each time there is even a distance suggestion of downfall, of impoverishment of life, of impotence, dissolution, decay, the aesthetic human being reacts with a No. Ugliness has a depressive impact, it is the expression of depression/dejection. It gains power, it impoverishes, it deadens.[5]

Art is always beautiful, because it affirms the life force of the human being, strengthens her physical and mental constitution;

---

4 Nietzsche, *Zur Genealogie der Moral*, VOL. 13, p. 228. See also p. 432: 'Beauty should not be a matter of taste for you, but a hunger: your need should mean beauty, or else I will have nothing to say to you.'

5 Nietzsche, *Zur Genealogie der Moral*, VOL. 13, p. 296. See also p. 499: 'All that is ugly weakens and afflicts the human being; it reminds her of decay, endangerment, powerlessness. One can measure the impression of ugliness with a dynamometer. Wherever there is oppression, there is ugliness. The feeling of power, the will to power, it grows in the presence of beauty, and declines in the face of ugliness.'

it is life-enhancing and stimulating, and reinforces the human being's will to power. The problem of a not-beautiful art does not arise in Nietzsche because he only sees art in its effect: that which oppresses human beings is ugly, and because it is ugly, it is not art.

Art enables life, gives the human being the strength to engage with life, to want to deal with it and to live it with enthusiasm: 'Art and nothing but art. It is life's great enabler, seducer, stimulant'.[6] And '[b]eauty and art can be directly attributed to many a diverse desire'.[7]

Based on its impact, Nietzsche conceptualizes art as a force contrary to a 'bleak view of the world':

> The conception of the world underlying this book is peculiarly grim and unpleasant: among the types of pessimism known so far, none has achieved this level of perniciousness. A true and visible world as a counterpart is altogether absent: there is only one world, and it is cruel, contradictory, beguiling, without meaning [. . .] a world like that is the real world [. . .] and we need lies in order to prevail upon this reality, this "truth", to live [. . .] That the lie is necessary in order to live is itself a part of this terrible and questionable character of existence.[8]

Nietzsche identifies art with lies. However, he also believes that 'metaphysics, morality, religion, science [are taken into account] as different forms of the lie: with their help it is possible to believe in life'.[9] The impossibility of knowledge gives

---

6 Nietzsche, *Zur Genealogie der Moral*, VOL. 13, p. 194.

7 Nietzsche, *Zur Genealogie der Moral*, VOL. 8, p. 432.

8 Nietzsche, *Zur Genealogie der Moral*, VOL. 13, p. 193.

9 Nietzsche, *Zur Genealogie der Moral*, VOL. 13, p. 193.

rise to art: 'We do not know the true nature of singular causality. Absolute scepticism: the need for art and illusion.'[10] What separates art from other kinds of lies is its life-enhancing power. As the great stimulant of life, art is greater than any so-called truth.[11]

Although the distinction between ugly and beautiful art falls away (in that, there is no such thing as ugly art), Nietzsche does introduce an internal differentiation, which, viewed from the standpoint of reception, is parallel to the differentiation between beauty and the sublime. Since it only evokes 'beautiful feelings',[12] beauty need not be the artist's primary concern. In fact, the artist should be far more concerned about the 'grand style', which exercises a power far beyond matters of taste:

> this style, like all great passions, disdains being liked; it forgets to persuade; that it commands, it wishes to [. . .] become master of all the chaos that one is; to force the chaos into form: logical, simply unambiguous; to become mathematics; to become a law—this is its great ambition.[13]

Art, which is identical with the will to power, is the transgression of the merely human,[14] of what is simply pleasing, of

---

10 Nietzsche, *Zur Genealogie der Moral*, VOL. 7, p. 458.

11 Nietzsche, *Zur Genealogie der Moral*, VOL. 13, p. 227.

12 Nietzsche, *Zur Genealogie der Moral*, VOL. 13, p. 247: 'The greatness of the artist cannot be measured according to the "beautiful feelings" that the artist evokes: that belief may be left to the women.'

13 Nietzsche, *Zur Genealogie der Moral*, VOL. 13, p. 247.

14 Nietzsche, *Zur Genealogie der Moral*, VOL. 13, p. 487: 'The few or the many of us who dare to live in a demoralised world, us heathens, live by the belief that we are perhaps the first to have understood what a pagan belief is: having to imagine ourselves as beings greater than the human being, as beings beyond good and evil.'

that which evokes 'beautiful feelings'. Great style forces chaos, 'that one is', in a form which has the clarity of mathematical and principled formulation. The sublime, which for Kant was a faculty located in the mind, to conceive of a transgression of one's own nature, now culminates in the work of art as a consequence of the human will to assume a form. This form unites necessity and lawfulness. It is the human being who overcomes her own chaos and gives herself the laws of form in the work of art. The faculty of play, which in the case of Schiller is the testimonial to being fully human, is only a superficial, laughable preoccupation in comparison with the re-creation of life, to which form must be given: 'One must not play with artistic formulae: one must recreate life itself so that it later formulates itself.'[15] The law does not tolerate play.

Nietzsche breaks away from the differentiation between appearance and truth, because he sees truth as an anthropological necessity, as a biologically useful construction that arises from human needs. The production of truth lends the chaos of the world a semblance of order and sense so that the human being is able to come to terms with the world that she has herself structured. The human being needs 'the supportive scaffolding of concepts' and of categories: 'Categories are "truths" only insofar as they are the preconditions of life: just as Euclidean space is a similarly defined "truth"'. This logic serves the purpose of 'imposing as much regularity and form as serves our practical needs'.[16]

If the world is the sum of statements made about it, and if these statements are owed to the biological need to impose a

---

15 Nietzsche, *Zur Genealogie der Moral*, VOL. 13, p. 132.

16 Nietzsche, *Zur Genealogie der Moral*, VOL. 13, p. 337, p. 888, p. 888, p. 334 and p. 333, respectively.

sense of regulatedness on disorder, then there is the impossibility of distinguishing between true and false statements. In place of establishing a distinction between truth and falsehood, Nietzsche establishes a distinction between that form of a lie which the world has rejected, and that form of a lie that the world affirms as a stimulant for life. Enduring pessimism is necessary to find; in the end, what is stronger than pessimism and 'more divine than the truth'[17] is art. Truth and lies, like appearance and reality, are indistinguishable. Thus, according to Nietzsche, after the elimination of this distinction, the task is to redefine value with a view to enhancing vitality or the will to power: 'We are faced with a problem of economy'.[18]

The value of art is measured according to its ability to teach human beings to affirm the world. There are three ways in which it has the task of deliverance:

> In this case, art serves as the only superior counterforce to all the will to negate life. [. . .] It is the salvation of the knower, of the one who witnesses, wishes to see the fearsome and questionable character of life, of the tragic knower. It is the salvation of the one who acts, of the one who not only sees the fearsome and questionable character of life, but lives it, wishes to live it, the tragic human being, the hero. It is the salvation of the one who suffers—as a path to conditions where suffering is desired, glorified, deified, where suffering is a form of rapture.[19]

---

17 See also Nietzsche, *Zur Genealogie der Moral*, VOL. 13, p. 500: 'Truth is ugly: we have art so that we do not perish in the face of reality.'

18 Nietzsche, *Zur Genealogie der Moral*, VOL. 13, p. 370.

19 Nietzsche, *Zur Genealogie der Moral*, VOL. 13, p. 226.

It is only art that can act as a counterpoint to the denial of life. As grand style indifferent to any questions about formal disposition, art can liberate humankind—it is capable of teaching the human being to affirm existence even in its tragic form as pain.[20] Art as will to power teaches the human being caught in the 'scaffolding of concepts' to recognize the tragic condition of being, transcending pain to the point of ecstasy, and transcending her own existence to achieve heroism. Art alone represents the force that can counteract the denial of life, a force that can save the human being from nihilism. 'And whenever the human being rejoices, she is the same in her joy, she is joyful in being an artist, takes pleasure in her power, enjoys the lie as her power'.[21]

What Kant allows as a consequence of pleasure in the presence of beauty—namely, a growing interest in the continued existence of the object of pleasure and the 'intensification of the feeling of being alive'—becomes for Nietzsche the very goal of art. Where Kant sees an objective purposefulness in using defining judgement, Nietzsche sees perspectivity determined by biological necessity, the results of which, irrespective of whether they are located in the area of knowledge, religion, metaphysics or art, cannot be distinguished categorically: they are a construction of the human mind in its need for order and regularity. Art sets itself apart under these practices of creating the world, because it was never seen as anything other than the production of appearance, and can never be seen as anything else because it carries within itself the principle of the construction of appearance undeniably limited by perspective; it is nothing but appearance, and to that extent not as deceptive as other forms of construction of the world which claim to be a part of the

---

20 Nietzsche, *Zur Genealogie der Moral*, VOL. 13, p. 241: 'Art affirms. Job affirms.'

21 Nietzsche, *Zur Genealogie der Moral*, VOL. 13, p. 521.

production of truth in contrast to the production of appearance. Nietzsche does not separate the spheres of appearance and reality, of subjective generality and objectivity, of autonomy and heteronomy. Rather, he is more concerned with reclaiming the real world after it has split into the doubly illusory,[22] in order to recover the unity of being, undivided by dialectic.

That appearance and reality were accorded the same status in the case of Fichte and Schelling had its own reasons in holding the I as absolute;[23] in Nietzsche, it acquires an epistemological turn, whereby, in the case that all knowledge is a matter of perspective, and rests on 'appearance, art, deception, optics, necessity of perspectivism and error',[24] appearance can then no longer distinguish itself categorically from reality.[25]

As everything is appearance, the distinction between art and reality, lie and truth, and true and false makes no sense. If it is not possible to arrive at a certain standpoint of disinterestedness, given that all knowledge is perspectival and any perspective is determined by the will to survival, one can only judge the various interests as per their respective value. In this 'economy', it is the will to power, the ability to affirm existence in all its forms, the very affirmation of life, that constitute the highest value; art in its intensity, in its direct tonal impact on the body,

---

22 Nietzsche, *Zur Genealogie der Moral*, VOL. 13, p. 24: 'The "real world", no matter how one has conceptualised it, was always the illusory world all over again.'

23 See Odo Marquard, *Aesthetica and Anaesthetica* (1989) (Munich: Fink, 2003), p. 111: 'In the case where the system of identities, as in the case of the Gesamtkunstwerk considered art and reality as being identical [...], reality itself takes on the qualities of illusion; and then art has everything that reality has, but reality no longer has anything to do with reality.'

24 Nietzsche, *Zur Genealogie der Moral*, VOL. 1, p. 18.

25 On the blurring of the boundaries of the aesthetic in Nietzsche, see Walter Ch. Zimmerli, 'Alles ist Schein' in Willi Oelmüller (ed.), *Kolloquium Kunst und Philosophie 2: Ästhetischer Schein* (Munich: Paderborn, 1982), p. 159.

is a medium of this affirmation and the counterforce to the denial of life.

In place of an aesthetic, Nietzsche develops a morality of art. There is no access to its manifestations, that is, works of art, that is specific to art. They demand (or deserve) no specific form of reflection about their integrity as artefacts or results of an activity that is appropriate to its end and finds its goal within itself. That which is conducive to happiness is art, and all that is art is conducive to happiness.

Nietzsche's erasure of the difference between reality and appearance, true and false, corresponds to an erasure of the difference between art and life. If the conception of the real world was so far a doubling of the world as appearance, then the erasure of the difference between appearance and reality in order to reclaim the real world must follow naturally. However, the erasure of aesthetic difference is synonymous with the replacing of aesthetics by morality. The problem of illusoriness of art, which became virulent following Schiller's critique of beauty as make-believe, is solved by Nietzsche as he generalizes appearance, and allows the world as product of necessary perspectives to disappear behind the perspective that has created the world in the first place.

EXCURSUS I: ON SEMBLANCE

Nietzsche's view of art marks a turning point in two ways. He puts an end to the conflict between truth and appearance, as well as to the critique of art that views it as an affirmation or even duplication of appearance. The roots of this critique can be traced back to Plato, who, as is well known, excludes the painter in participating in the truth by naming the painter an imitator of appearance (*Politeia* 597). If the visible world is appearance, then art as imitation of the appearance of objects in the medium of appearance is twice as reprehensible. Plato goes on to add that the painter understands nothing of what she represents (Plato demonstrates this through the example of the carpenter, whose work the painter does not understand). The artist thus deceives the uneducated (women and children), whereas the learned person is able to see through this deception.

Plato argues against art because it represents the visible world only mimetically. Art cannot be identified with the question of truth since its objects, as being illusory, fall prey to the verdict of deceptiveness. So long as art creates the startling effect of *imitatio*,[1] it cannot be compatible with philosophy,

---

1 See Ernst Kris, Otto Kurz, *Die Legende vom Künstler. Ein geschichtlicher Versuch* (1934) (Frankfurt am Main: Suhrkamp Verlag, 1980), p. 90ff.

which concerns itself primarily with truth, and appearance can never be truth.

Art can forge different relationships with its own deceptive character and with what can be viewed as truth. As long as reality is not seen as being identical with the visible world, art is free of the task of representing reality. The image is neither true nor false, but merely a reference, an analogon, rooted in the visible world, to something which in principle is beyond visibility. The appearance of the image is a reflection in the same way as the appearance of light is the reflection of the divine. In the case of Abbot Suger,[2] unlike in Plato, appearance is not a bleak shadow but, rather, an allegory for participation in the complexity of a system of references as it unfolds, in that which transcends all knowledge. It is not material objects that cast shadows that are mistaken for the truth by some. Rather, appearance represents an entity that, in principle, both eludes and transcends understanding, a being which appears in the light that breaks upon the material object. The object is the medium of light just as the light is the medium of appearance. The path of this light is neither something that has to be reconstructed mathematically, as in the case of Dürer, nor is it a matter of looking through, of perspective.[3] Rather, it is one of 'seeing through' in the sense of diaphaneity.[4]

---

2 See Erwin Panofsky, 'Abt Suger von St. Denis' in *Sinn und Deutung in der bildenden Kunst* (1946/1955) (Cologne: Dumont Verlag, 1975), pp. 125–66.

3 Erwin Panofsky, 'Perspective als symbolische Form' (1927) in Hariolf Oberer and Egon Verheyen (eds), *Aufsätze zu Grundfragen der Kunstwissenschaft* (Berlin: Hessling, 1974), pp. 99–168.

4 See Hans Sedlmayr, *Die Entstehung der Kathedrale* (1950) (Freiburg: Herder, 1993), p. 604: 'The sensual light is no longer a symbol, but an image (imago) of the true, intelligible light.' Here, Sedlmayr quotes Abbot Suger, who, *more anagogico*, transposed the material on the non-material: 'The weak spirit rises to truth through the material, and through the light it

49

❀

There is another way of relating to the world that is seen in the writings of theoreticians of Italian mannerism, for whom *inventio* is more important than *imitatio*, that is, mimesis.[5] At the outset, the claim of *adaequatio* as the claim on the revelation of truth is given up in favour of *disegno interno*,[6] the inner image in its dubitability, its questionability, in fact, in its very unfoundability, which the artist equates with the image of the visible external world. Art is thus no longer a practice of representation but a practice of exploring possibilities. It thereby distances itself from the claim of rules imposed on it externally; laws of form inherent to the work of art suffice to justify the work of art with the conviction that with the artist a spark of divine ingenuity is at work, that created the cosmos. This allows the artist a near-divine freedom from the demand to simply recreate

---

longingly rises out of its declivity' (p. 240f.). See also the reference to Duns Scotus whose work Suger is said to have studied, and who 'counted works of art as part of "materialia" that that can reflect the "immaterialia"' (p. 600). 'The work of art is a vehicle that leads the observer "per visibilia ad invisibilia".' (p. 605).

5 See Erwin Panofsky, *Idea. Ein Beitrag zur Begriffsgeschichte der älteren Kunsttheorie* (1924) (Berlin: Teubner, 1989). 'Imitatio' and 'inventio' can be considered as parallel to the 'theory of imitation and to the concept of ideas. See p. 71: 'In some ways, the contradiction between the "theory of ideas" and the "theory of imitation" in art theory is similar to the epistemological opposition between the "theory of the image" and "conceptualism" [...]: in both cases, the relation of the subject with regard to the object is quickly interpreted either as a purely reproductive representation, or in the sense of a productive activity, based on "inherent ideas" [...]. [We believe we have recognised] that the artistic perspective is as rarely confronted with the 'thing in itself' as discerning reason is. Rather it can be certain of the validity of its results precisely because it defines—as reason does—the rules of its own world itself.'

6 Federico Zuccari, *L'Idea de' Pittori, Scultori e Architetti* (Torino, 1607) in Detlef Heikamp (ed.), *Scritti d'Arte di Federico Zuccaro* (Florence: L. S. Oslchki, 1961), p. 95.

reality as appearance. The primacy given to the *disegno interno* and the *inventio* over the *imitatio* frees the work of art from its duty with respect to the heteronomous.

This is where the autonomy of the work in thinking about art comes into play, with the development of an art market, the emergence of the artist as entrepreneur who makes his services available, and is accompanied by the oft-discussed emancipation of art from the restrictions and requirements set by a feudal and ecclesiastical clientele. It is these forces—gentrification, the establishment of an art market, diversification of societies that can be classified according to different subsystems, functionally, rather than stratificationally, popularization of the cult of genius, and a flattened and therefore broad reception of the image of the *divino artista*—that lead to the all-too-familiar scenario: on the one hand, the royalty of the art world, such as Makart, Lenbach and Böcklin, who enjoyed the sort of reverence from their contemporaries in ways hardly comprehensible today. On the other hand, the emergence of the dandy who holds up his *ennui* before a society he despises.[7] Both these types derive their legitimacy from their elitist self-image. While one constitutes the self through recourse to a past whose promises they fulfil and even surpass (for instance, Thoma as the new Dürer),[8] conforming to the system of the *imitatio*, both of the old and of nature, the other resort to the *topos* of the avant-garde, which is in the long run far more attractive and

---

7 See Henning Mehnert, *Melancholie und Inspiration: begriffs- und wissenschaftsgeschichtliche Untersuchungen zur poetisches 'Psychologie' Baudelaires, Flauberts und Mallarmés. Mit einer Studie über Rabelais* (Heidelberg: C. Winter, 1978), p. 143 ff.

8 See Henry Thode, *Böcklin und Thoma. Acht Vorträge über neudeutsche Malerei gehalten für ein Gesamtpublikum an der Universität Heidelberg 1905* (Heidelberg: Carl Winter's Universitatsbuchhandlung, 1905).

claims, by definition, to be a step ahead.[9] Being secure in the recourse to the past loses its value when compared with the ability to look into a future the masses do not yet know of.

The burden of the autonomy that art experiences at this moment, because it has become the avant- garde, has a new quality. All supportive contexts are demolished, all frames of reference dispelled, every relationality is rejected. While the Impressionists sought to anchor the subjectivization of the gaze by way of objectivization through reference to the natural sciences and anatomy, the singularity of subjectivity now becomes a compulsion. The only thing that can be tolerated is a kind of inner necessity.[10] That this too must be communicated intersubjectively is emphasized in the manifestos published by the Brücke artists as well as by the Munich-based artists of the Blaue Reiter group. The subjectivization of art requires that it produces its own contexts: programmes, pamphlets, manifestos, interpretations.[11] The Impressionists are pioneers on that count as well because they tried to counteract the isolation of the artist caused by the subjectivization of her practice by declaring it to be socially relevant.[12] The production of texts accompanying the production of images can, on the whole, be considered a phenomenon symptomatic of modernity, and the first proponent of this practice can be said to be Vasari.[13] After all, it is

9 See Peter Bürger, *Theorie der Avantgarde* (Frankfurt am Main: Suhrkamp Verlag, 1974).

10 Wassily Kandinsky, *Über das Geistige in der Kunst* (1912) (Bern: Benteli, 1979), with an Introduction by Max Bill.

11 See Arnold Gehlen, *Zeitbilder* (Frankfurt am Main: Athenaum Verlag, 1960).

12 See Thomas Crow, 'Moderne und Massenkultur in der bildenden Kunst', *Texte zur Kunst* 1 (1990): 48 and 83n4.

13 Giorgio Vasari, *Lebensgeschichten der berühmtesten Maler, Bildhauer und Architekten* (Ernst Jaffé ed.), (Zürich: Diogenes Verlag, 1980[1568]).

Vasari who puts an end to the confusingly contradictory usage of the concept of modernity by associating with modernity the art of the Renaissance that he so greatly praised and propagated.[14] This marks the beginning of the idea that modernity isn't simply what is happening now but that which refers to the future.

The autonomization of the work of art, which begins with the introduction of *inventio* as a defining category of artistic endeavour and leads to inner necessity as in Kandinsky, could not, as stated earlier, be imagined without the so-called philosophy of unity[15] in the early Romantics and the ennoblement of semblance in Nietzsche. This marks a break in the association of art with the world. No longer weighed down by indebtedness to an object, the principle of *adaequatio,* only if yet another principle is needed, is replaced by the principle of analogy or correlation.

Freed of its duty to perform mimesis, art can not only choose its form and object but also choose, ideally, to entirely abandon form and object. The work of art, when completed, needs no correlation with an object which is not identical to it. The work becomes a *fait pictorial*, of the same value as any other object in the world, pure appearance without referentiality.[16]

---

14 Erwin Panofsky, *Die Renaissancen der europäischen Kunst* (1960) (Frankfurt am Main: Suhrkamp Verlag, 1979), p. 46ff.

15 Klaus Lankheit, *Die Frühromantik und die Grundlagen der 'gegenstandslosen' Malerei* in *Neue Heidelberger Jahrbücher* (Heidelberg, New York, G. Koester, 1951), pp. 55–90. For an analysis of Lankheit's arguments, see Peter Anselm Riedl, 'Kandinsky und die Tradition' in *Heidelberger Jahrbücher* (Heidelberg, New York: Springer, 1978), pp. 3–17.

16 See Karl Ruhrberg, Klaus Honnef, Manfred Schneckenburger, Christiane Fricke and Ingo F. Walther, *Art of the 20th Century*, VOL. 1 (Cologne: Taschen, 2000), p. 354. See also Kristine Stiles, Peter Howard Selz (eds), *Theories and Documents of Contemporary Art* (Berkeley: University of California Press, 1996), p. 113f., p. 117.

This centripetal aspect of autonomous art leads to the series of inquiries in search of the fundamental principles of artistic practice and design: the horizontal, the vertical, primary colours, the pure sinus wave, sound, light and so forth. Art thus delves into itself in search of something that inquirers hope will be the ineluctable cause behind all art.

The fact that mimesis no longer determines form allows for all kinds of form to be declared as art. The nominalism of the art of the twentieth century is not limited to declaring *objets trouvés* as artefacts; the expansion of the field of art through the integration of different art forms beyond the concept of art, with art made by children or those with mental illness signifies a moment of a centrifugal process of the expansion of the arts which has continued unflaggingly since the beginning of the twentieth century. From that moment on, any declaration that something is art, has to be believed.

The subjectivist rhetoric of sensitivity and synaesthesia of a Kandinsky is countered by the Dadaists with nonsense, by the futurists with the call to destroy everything that can be looked upon as culture, by the Surrealists with gratuitous acts of violence.[17] The centripetal pull towards autonomy for which the work of art is everything is countered by the centrifugal movement towards the erasure of aesthetic difference for which art is nothing. Once again, art is mere appearance that ought to be done away with, a component of a false reality that must disappear along with it. Autonomous art, separated from life, represents a break in the social continuum, the wound of alienation that must be closed up.

---

17 André Breton, *Zweites Manifest des Surrealismus* (1930), in *Die Manifeste des Surrealismus* (Reinbek bei Hamburg: Rowohlt, 1986), p. 56.

In Germany, the centrifugal movement towards the expansion of the concept of art and the blurring of boundaries between the arts culminates in the work of Joseph Beuys, whose repeated participation in the documenta elevated him to the stature of a world-artist in the eyes of the German art establishment, whereas other national artistic milieus saw him as a German exception or took no note of him. Even if one would like to ignore him to some extent, given especially the pseudo-religious brouhaha around him in Germany, his position remains central to this argument simply because of the strength of the reception of his work. His practice and the texts that accompanied his practice absolutize art as total praxis; every element of the social becomes a part of the totality of art, which dissolves them more than it integrates them. There remains only one force that drives the social: creativity. And art only has one goal: first, to prevent the destruction of human life, and second, to build human life. Only this is art, and nothing else.[18]

Beuys' announced exit from the art world in 1985 indicates that he simultaneously maintained two views of art: one emphatic and the other descriptive. There is a false art, which one must step away from, whereas the emphatic view refers to the kind of art that seeks to build human life. This bipolarity in speaking of art reflects the difference between the idea of art and the work of art. It is possible to produce works of art that critique the supposedly established view of art, in fact in relation to the centrifugal expansion of the idea of art it is practically the duty of art to question the idea of art through the work of art. Only that which subverts the idea of art is art. Avant-garde art, which must constantly cross the boundaries of the

---

18 Joseph Beuys, *Nur Dieses ist Kunst*, [o. J.] 11.4 x 16.2 cm, Joseph Beuys estate. See Kirsten Claudia Voigt, '"Artivismus", Pragmatismus und Narrativierung' in *Kunstforum International* 231 (February–March 2015): 58.

idea of art if it wishes to live up to its definition, sees itself confronted with the problem which led Duchamp to the question:
'Is it possible to create works that are not works of art?'[19] While
Duchamp certainly is concerned with art that is not artistry,
whose cunning lies in testing the tenacity of the 'frame effect',[20]
Beuys believes that the framework of what can be described as
art can be endlessly extended to be able to organise life itself
according to the power of creativity. Both trajectories of conceptual struggle may, in the end, have a meeting point: for
Beuys, aesthetic difference disappears because life reorders itself
according to art; it also disappears for Duchamp because ultimately ways were found to create works of art that were no
longer art.

---

19 Calvin Tomkins, *Marcel Duchamp* (1997) (Munich: Hanser Verlag,
1999), p. 157.

20 Erving Goffmann, *Rahmen-Analyse* (1974) (Frankfurt am Main:
Suhrkamp Verlag, 1977).

Nietzsche II

Tying up art with the task of redeeming the world has been a part of Nietzsche's work and that of the rhetoric of the art world since the mid-twentieth century, but with varying indicators. For Nietzsche, art is the only true medium of redemption; art as forced appearance surpasses the illusoriness of a world that, constructed through a multiplicity of perspectives, remains undiscoverable in and on account of most of these equally valid but mutually contradictory perspectives. Art functions as the greatest stimulant of life, a revitalizing tonic that penetrates deep into the very musculature of human beings. All rhetoric about art in the postmodern uses a similar terminology, and yet approaches the question of the appropriateness of the task given to art from the other end. While for Nietzsche art was 'the only possibility of life'[1] and human existence was only justifiable aesthetically,[2] now it is a question of justifying art. So that, should art continue to exist, it must perform all the work of building humanity—and this alone, nothing else.

---

1 Nietzsche, *Zur Genealogie der Moral*, VOL. 7, p. 76.
2 Nietzsche, *Zur Genealogie der Moral*, VOL. 10, p. 238.

What binds Nietzsche and the relational aesthetic[3] beyond these differences is the perception that the value of art is based on the contribution it makes towards a better life and towards creating and maintaining human dignity. Art as the art of centrifugal transgression is relevant to the relational aesthetic only in terms of what it produces as social value. In the case of participatory art, this manifests as direct intervention in the social fabric, in the theories of Bourriaud as a model for better social coexistence towards which a society must orient itself.

Should one characterize the discussion on the relation between ideas connoted in 'appearance' and 'reality' as a discussion on the value of aesthetics and morals, then it seems that morals constantly extend their scope. The arts may occupy forms and discrete areas which had so far not been seen as appropriately worthy of art and contribute to the revaluation of values through processes of profanation and valorization.[4] However, these processes initiate less an enhancement of scope of the aesthetic than they do a validity of morals. The blurring of the boundaries of art serves the pushing back of the aesthetic as a system of differentiation between beauty and ugliness. This differentiation, which Schiller critiqued in his deprecation of art as little more than a thing of service to humankind, and the not-beautiful, the sublime, which he lauded as the only thing worthy of tragic humanity, becomes less important in Nietzsche who casts out of the realm of art all that is both pleasing and ugly, all that weakens the will, as being of little value, and only allows that which is empowering to be seen as beautiful.

---

3 See Nicolas Bourriaud, *Relational Aesthetics* (Simon Pleasance & Fronza Woods trans, with Mathieu Copeland) (Dijon: Les presses du reel, 2002).

4 See Boris Groys, *Über das Neue* (Munich: Hanser Verlag, 1992).

This twofold codification and revaluation of concepts in Nietzsche also applies to appearance. As he says, 'To my mind [to me], the first [immediate] solution was the aesthetic justification of human existence. However: "justification" need not be necessary at all! Morality belongs in the realm of appearance.'[5]

The reference to morals as belonging, like art, in the realm of the illusory, contradicts the impulse to justify being in aesthetic terms. A little later, however, he refers to 'redemption through appearance'.[6] As a result, there are two forms of appearance: as redemption (as a 'vision'); and as a lie. Appearance as surpassing the appearance of reality and thus the manifestation of truth over the illusoriness of the real on the one hand, and as distortion of the real, as a muddying of reality, on the other. In this paradoxical deployment of concepts, Nietzsche finds a way to produce monosemantics. In this manner, aesthetic appearance is celebrated as redemption, even though it is equally about transcending art: 'In place of the genius, I prefer the human being, who transcends herself to overcome being human—a new concept of art (against the art of works of art).'[7] The new concept of art is the concept of life as art, of a life that replaces the idea of art by surpassing the very power to transcend life. In the end, the redemptive power of art frees art from itself; it is art beyond art. The unconditional belief in redemption through appearance leads to the elimination of the idea of the work of art and to the blurring of its boundaries. Life itself becomes a work of art as an avenue to avail of the promise of

---

5 Nietzsche, *Zur Genealogie der Moral*, VOL. 10, p. 238. He mentions earlier that he has always been concerned with proving the innocence of becoming and with upholding the independence of praise or censure in the present in order 'to follow goals oriented towards the future of humankind.'

6 Nietzsche, *Zur Genealogie der Moral*, VOL. 10, p. 238.

7 Nietzsche, *Zur Genealogie der Moral*, VOL. 10, p. 503.

happiness and redemption held by appearance. The human being as creator, the artist, no longer creates works of art. Rather, she creates the human being who does away with herself in unshackling herself from being merely human, and in doing so, recreates herself 'as a being beyond good and evil',[8] and thus leads to a new idea of art as the new idea of being human.

8 Nietzsche, *Zur Genealogie der Moral*, VOL. 13, p. 487.

Hegel: Decision, Diremption, Freedom

In Hegel, we find a detailed discussion on the broadening of the concept of art, artistic transgressions, and their ability to expand into terrain hitherto unexplored or closed off, and to appropriate any material it has access to:[1]

> Bondage to a particular subject-matter and a mode of portrayal suitable for this material alone are for artists today something past, and art therefore has become a free instrument which the artist can wield in proportion to his subjective skill in relation to any material of whatever kind. [. . .] No content, no form, is any longer immediately identical with the inwardness, the nature, the unconscious substantial essence of the artist; every material may be indifferent to him if only it does not contradict the formal law of being simply beautiful and capable of artistic treatment. Today there is no material that stands in and for itself above this relativity, and even if one matter be raised above it, still there is no absolute need for its representation by art.
>
> [. . .] in this way every form and every material is now at the service and command of the artist whose

---

1 Georg Wilhelm Friedrich Hegel, *Aesthetics: Lectures on Fine Art*, VOLS 1 & 2 (T. M. Knox trans.) (Oxford: Clarendon Press, 1975).

talent and genius is explicitly freed from the earlier limitation to one specific art form.[2]

Hegel articulates the possibility that art would move towards the unknown, beyond any limits that a normative aesthetic would seek to impose upon it, and would subject the known to a transformation both with respect to its content and its form. Beauty as the 'pure appearance of the Idea to sense'[3] thus does not somehow imply an 'idealistic aesthetics',[4] but upholds the relationality of the work of art to that which it is not. In the emergence of the Idea, the difference between the object and its appearance is maintained. Beauty consists in the truth with which the work of art, which is always a part of the realm of appearance as the realm of not-truth, reveals it. Appearance as different from the truth actually reveals the truth, and it is in this representational revelation that art finds its justification.

Hegel distances himself from the idea that 'art has to serve as a means to moral purposes, and the moral end of the world in general, by instructing and improving, and thus has its substantial aim not in itself, but in something else'.[5] Despite his critique of

---

2 Hegel, *Aesthetics*, VOL. 1, p. 605 and p. 606.

3 Hegel, *Aesthetics*, VOL. 1, p. 157. See also pp. 91–2: 'But beauty is only a specific way of expressing and representing the true, and therefore stands open throughout in every respect to conceptual thinking, so long as that thinking is actually equipped with the power of the Concept. [. . .] For beauty, as was said already [. . .] is no such abstraction of the Understanding but the inherently concrete absolute Concept and, more specifically, the absolute Idea in its appearance in a way adequate to itself.'

4 See also Hegel, *Aesthetics*, VOL. 1, p. 161: 'But out of this recognition there has arisen a mania for ideal representation in which people believed they had found beauty, but it lapsed into flatness, lifelessness, and superficiality without character.'

5 Hegel, *Aesthetics*, VOL. 1, p. 55

Kant,[6] the work of art is preserved in its autonomy, subject to its own laws, and exists in continuing to find its purpose in itself.

The ability that art possesses, according to Hegel, to occupy any subject matter and to use every form, every material that can be opened up to artistic engagement, has its price. Since the end of classical art, it is no longer the privileged medium which reveals the truth. 'For us art counts no longer as the highest mode in which truth fashions an existence for itself'.[7]

The end of art in its function as the bearer of truth[8] is not the end of all art—after all, art can well achieve new heights[9]—but rather the end of its immediacy and the necessity of the appearance of truth through the medium of art. The spirit, which no longer has art as its greatest need, turns to truth. That truth is necessarily revealed in art as beauty is a matter of the past.[10] All that the work of art now evokes in being observed is pleasure and critical judgement.

---

6 Hegel, *Aesthetics*, VOL. 1, pp. 56–60.

7 Hegel, *Aesthetics*, VOL. 1, p. 103.

8 Hegel, *Aesthetics*, VOL. 1, p. 50: 'In all these respects art, considered in its highest vocation, is and remains for us a thing of the past. Thereby it has lost for us genuine truth and life and has rather been transferred into our *ideas* instead of maintaining its earlier necessity in reality and occupying its higher place.' See also Christian Demand, *Die Beschämung der Philister* (Springe: Klampen Verlag, 2007), p. 18 ff.

9 See also Hegel, *Aesthetics*, VOL. 1, p. 103: 'We may well hope that art will always rise higher an come to perfection, but the form of art has ceased to be the supreme need of the spirit. No matter how excellent we find the statues of the Greek gods, no matter how we see God the Father, Christ, and Mary so estimably and perfect portrayed: it is no help; we bow the knee no longer.'

10 Hegel, *Aesthetics*, VOL. 1, p. 535: 'But if it is a matter of the consciousness of *truth, then the beauty* of the appearance, and of the representation, is an accessory and rather indifferent, for the truth is present for consciousness independently of art.'

❈

HEGEL

This uncoupling of beauty and truth is the appearance of a truth with reference to the mode of existence of a bourgeois society, with the truth of diremption as its signature.[11] Diremption is the precondition for the existence of the spirit that seeks its own objective existence which, as its own object, dirempts within itself.[12] It is the work of the spirit which becomes the work of the consciousness that grants freedom to itself, to split into its own object and its continued existence.[13] The spirit that turns itself into a work is simultaneously what it is, only in that it becomes.[14] It represents within itself the separation between its becoming and its being,[15] between its acting in itself and its object, between the 'in itself' and the 'for itself', between consciousness and self-consciousness.

---

11 Georg Friedrich Wilhelm Hegel, *Elements of the Philosophy of Right* (H. B. Nisbet trans.) (Cambridge: Cambridge University Press, 2003[1991]), p. 62: 'But the ethical substance is likewise *natural* spirit—the family, in its *division* and *appearance—civil society*' In *Aesthetics*, VOL. I, p. 197, Hegel refers to the 'monster of disunion'.

12 See Hegel, *Aesthetics*, VOL. 1, p. 187, pp. 225-6.

13 Georg Friedrich Wilhelm Hegel, *The Phenomenology of Spirit* (Terry Pinkard trans.) (Cambridge: Cambridge University Press, 2018).

14 Hegel, *The Phenomenology of Spirit*, p. 462: 'However, this substance, which is spirit, is its *coming-to-be* what it, the substance, is *in itself*; and it is as this coming-to be which is taking a reflective turn into itself that spirit is truly in itself *spirit*. Spirit is in itself the movement which is cognition— the transformation of that former *in-itself* into *for-itself*, of *substance* into *subject*, of the object of consciousness into the object of *self-consciousness*, i.e. into an object that is just as much sublated, or into the *concept.*'

15 See also Georg Wilhelm Friedrich Hegel, *The Philosophy of History* (J. Sibree trans.) (New York: Dover Publications, 1956), p. 17: 'Two things must be distinguished in consciousness; first, the fact that I *know*; secondly, *what I know. In self* consciousness these are merged in one; for Spirit *knows itself.* It involves an appreciation of its own nature, as also an energy enabling it to realize itself; to make itself *actually* that which it is *potentially.*'

Modern bourgeois society as a society of diremption is also a society of subjects that have rights. These rights, the lawfulness of which every subject can insist upon—since the bourgeois subject is a subject that has the right to have rights—constitute the social as totality of the will of individuals as specific. The subjective right gives 'to *particularity* [. . .] the right to develop and express itself in all directions'.[16] It enables the totalization of the particular as the only category that can claim to be universally applicable.

Although the separation between the general and the particular[17] is not only a reflection of the complex intertwining interests of the subject and of society, which corresponds to the separation of society and nature, diremption is rooted far more firmly in the disposition of the subject itself. 'In other words, the "I" is simultaneously the most individual and the most universal [element]'.[18]

Just as the human being has emancipated and separated herself from nature, so too the bourgeois subject separates and emancipates itself from society. Its uniqueness separates it from society and all other subjects, and it shares with all other subjects this uniqueness and discontinuity. While such diremption may divide bourgeois society, it also unites all its members in the common characteristic they share of being separate from one another and from what really binds them together. The structure of diremption allows for a totality of subjectivity and generality, and with that the generality of the rights of all subjects in their uniqueness, distinctness and differentiation, which, as the totality of freedom, knows nothing outside it. In an

---

16 Hegel, *Elements of the Philosophy of Right*, p. 184, p. 221

17 Hegel, *Elements of the Philosophy of Right*, pp. 221–2.

18 Hegel, *Elements of the Philosophy of Right*, p. 275, p. 313.

overlap between subjective will and general will, owed to the fact that the rights of the subject to be different are placed at the heart of the process of the law, the social constitutes itself as the totality of the freedom of that which is different. The totality of freedom excludes the other, for or against which the subject may decide. Freedom as totality rescinds itself.

At the same time, diremption resists that the becoming consolidates itself as being. All that is in existence, as it exists, is only temporary. The 'monster of diremption' represents the process of the formation of the social in its paradoxical interlacing of subjectivity and generality as generality of subjectivity, of the erosion of the social and the production of the social as the difference within the social itself. Freedom as necessity answers, in itself, to the totality of freedom, which continually erases its own horizon and tolerates no limits, and to freedom as transgression of all its own certitudes as an intrinsically paradoxical form. Not only does freedom come up against limits to its very idea where it has no outside and poses as a contradiction to itself, it is also the totality of freedom that gives rise to a second contradiction within itself, namely, the coercion to freedom. The concordance between subjective will and general will hands over the subject to the power of the absolute coincidence of subjectivity and generality. Distancing itself from, contradicting and rejecting this absolute coincidence as the fruition of the general good amounts to a rejection of its own subjectivity by the subject which, precisely through its dissolution in the totality of the social, governed by subjectivity, can simultaneously renounce as well as preserve the difference, which separates itself from all other subjects. Rejecting such absolute coincidence is also the rejection of freedom and the denial of one's own mode of existence. The subject cannot but affirm the freedom in which the subject has created itself as the social along with other subjects. The coercion to agree to it corresponds with the totality of freedom.

At the same time, diremption, which in the first place has enabled subjectivity as the freedom of the subject from demands of society, creates within the totality of freedom the possibility of an Other to freedom, which diremption institutes as a freedom that contradicts itself. Just as that which exists can only demonstrate its existence temporarily, so too can freedom as total manifest itself only temporarily. The propensity to outwardly transgress boundaries, which means little more than the erasure of those horizons, their disappearance and the erection of a total inwardness for which there is nothing beyond, corresponds with the emergence of an ever-newer other within the totality of freedom. This other is not the opposite of freedom, it is not a coercion—it is, rather, a different form of freedom, a kind of freedom singularly forgotten, disparaged and devalued, and endowed with values yet again, equipped with new signs in an 'economy of values'. It is in keeping with the logic of diremption that, in due course, it simultaneously produces the other; that it always creates something to go with what is created. Something which, beyond the binary opposition, represents a hitherto empty or emptied possibility which will reveal itself at a particular, albeit unforeseeable, moment.

Diremption has no opposite. It sets in at the heart of social processes, with the smallest unit, the I, which embodies the middle of two extremes, the particular and the general. It is this smallest unit, which is divided as the centre of two poles and from which diremption as a social process is set in motion, as the becoming of the totality of freedom at the centre of which diremption keeps alive the possibility of another kind of freedom, which contradicts totality and consolidates it in one and the same movement. This movement is the movement of the mind, which constitutes itself both as the how and the what of its autonomy, of its own mobility, both as object and as means. It produces itself as its own object, and as the method for securing its object, as the consciousness of the 'firstly, that I know, and secondly, what I know'. In the activity of the mind, which constitutes itself as being and becoming, diremption manifests itself as a generative principle which shapes the mind into what it is as a foretaste of what it could be.

This permanence of division can be described as a parallel process of identification, and the production of the not-identified, as the process of revealing and the production of invisibility. Any attempt at differentiation can be termed as, first of all, acts of the mind. To then identify what it will engage with, the mind must isolate a form from matter, a shape from the unformed mass. In this process, it produces that which it identifies as its object and excludes that which does not hold its interest. It marks a part of reality as relevant and leaves that which it is not interested in unmarked. The compulsion to differentiate is unavoidable, because even the decision to not differentiate represents a differentiation between two options, the identification of two possibilities, one of which one must decide upon, the drawing of a line across the unmarked, which must decide between what can be marked and the unmarked.

The function of the mind, the production of difference, is a function in the world and occurs in this world. The mind does not operate beyond the world but within the field, the scope of which lies between the totality of freedom and its opposition, the totality of diremption which it sees as the generating principle that governs it. And the way in which it produces visibility and invisibility when it engages with the world produces its own blindness even as it sees.[19] In identifying objects

---

19 See George Spencer-Brown, *Laws of Form* (London: Allen and Unwin, 1979), p. 105: 'But in order to do so, evidently it [the world] must first cut

of its activity, with every form, it produces that which is unknown to it on the side of the object. Not only does what the unknown could be remains hidden from it, because the production of the unknown corresponds with the production of blindness, it is the unknown itself that remains hidden from it. It is only revealed to the mind as it reflects on its activity, that its observing the world produces visibility and darkness.[20]

The first differentiation is always incidental, because it cannot be consequential. What follows the initial differentiation develops logicality and consistency as a sequence in the development of forms, the observation of these forms and the communication about these observations. The isolated and defined forms repeat the form of differentiation, which separates it from the environment, in the process of further differentiation as a distinction within itself, as the production of new forms and invisibilities. It is through this autopoetic closure that forms acquire plausibility as being consistent in themselves and represent propositions in communication which prove to be viable, conclusive and useful in further communication. The apparent certainty of that which communication deals with and which it secures, whereby the observable refers to the observable, the observed to the observed, allows the fact to be forgotten that it is arbitrariness which cannot be separated from the schematizing and systematizing construction of reality that is at the bottom of decisions. Whatever the communication of observations

---

itself up into at least one state which sees, and at least one other state which is seen. In this severed and mutilated condition, whatever it sees is only partially itself. WE may take it that the world undoubtedly is itself (i.e. is indistinct from itself), but, in any attempt to see itself as an object, it must, equally undoubtedly, act so as to make itself distinct from, and therefore false to, itself. In this condition, it will always partially elude itself.'

20 See Niklas Luhmann, *Schriften zu Kunst und Literatur* (Frankfurt am Main: Suhrkamp Verlag, 2008), p. 192, p. 254.

leads to, and which world can be created through it, it remains, although it is to be presupposed, inaccessible.[21]

In representing itself as the totality of differentiations, the world is a possible but not a necessary, that is, a contingent world which appears as plausible in the communication about the observed differentiations. Observations gain value within communication not as statements that indicate their value through truthfulness but because they offer points of connectability for the process of further communication. The large number of points of connection and the development of longer chains of selection[22] across heterogenous contexts creates the impression that what is observed is a truth, removed from contingency and arbitrariness, embedded in an area in which the observation, that everything that can be said, is said by observers, is no longer valid.[23]

Such phenomena of plausibilization, which owe themselves to the development of consistency through feedback effects, to the re-entry of differentiation into the differentiated, to the reduction of complexity through the re-emergence of the observed in the first order into the observation of a second order, contribute towards reducing the complexity of observation.

The decision taken after the first differentiation, as an apparent merging of what was hitherto separate, becomes the basis upon which further decisions as links in a coherent chain

---

21 Luhmann, *Schriften*, p. 209: 'In every operation, the world continues to exist in its inaccessibility. It remains transcendentally presupposed. All operations are and remain operations in the world.'

22 Luhmann, *Schriften*, p. 32.

23 Humberto R. Maturana, *Erkennen: Die Organisation und Verkörperung von Wirklichkeit: Ausgewählte Arbeiten zur biologischen Epistemologie* (Braunschweig: Teubner Verlag, 1982), p. 34: 'Everything that can be said is said by an observer.'

❊

of conclusions can follow, which in their entirety tend to produce their own contexts. The totality of differentiations constitutes the environment of the individual differentiation, and this in turn must prove their internal integrity as well as their outward coherence as a system within an environment in relation to its outside, in relation to the multi-contextually constituted environment of all other observable systems of individual differentiations, their consistence and adaptability.

What Does Art Do after the End of Art?

Art is one of the forms that diremption takes as it unfolds. Art owes its end, its character as being irretrievably in the past, to a new freedom, a freedom it did not experience before, a freedom of access to means, themes, methods, processes and forms which enable it to complete the movement of permanent transgression which society performs. As a social subsystem, art is engulfed by the dynamics that govern it, contributing to the process of constant diversification. It expands at the same time as it constantly unfolds towards boundaries which it sets up in order only to transgress them. Freed of the need to produce truth, it produces within the world of contingency a world of analogous forms of possibilities, idiosyncratic and highly improbable propositions for communication which can nevertheless be utilized, processed further and sharpened, as well as rejected and strengthened. Like other form complexes of communication, art must work towards its own plausibilization. In the same measure, it is subject to the danger of disappearing if, as a subsystem, it is unable to prove its own insubstitutability with the plausibilization of its difference to other subsystems.

There seem to be two discernible methods through which art responds to the process of diremption, the loss of its own imperative, the gaining of its freedom, two ways in which it relates to the society within which it is situated, to its fate of no longer being entrusted with the task of leading to 'the absolute idea in its commensurate appearance'. For now, art is a form of social construction, freed of all compulsions and necessities, a possibility that allows for the development of other forms of the social within the social, other forms of freedom in the realm of freedom. However, the loss of necessity produces the need for justification. As in fact a medium of freedom, art must illustrate which reality it wishes to construct and which space it seeks to occupy in the world of a variety of plausible constructions, in the world of narratives, and why it seeks to do so, what value should be accorded to its production of appearance, and which unique achievement it brings to the system that no other subsystem is capable of.

One method is the reduction of complexity. In the realm of forced appearance, the work of art provides a model based on which the participant in the social can recognize the truth of her reality. In a sense, she looks beyond the boundary between reality and appearance towards this model, and from this vantage point draws conclusions about reality out of which perception takes place. The model has the advantage of a clarifying, simplifying, representation of the complex reality of the social. It demonstrates the ability of the artist to articulate a truth about the social, which otherwise would have remained hidden. She possesses a sensorium for the present, which distinguishes her from others, and enables her to bring to light the central structural elements of the real through an exemplificatory representation of reality.

The model which is based on a reduction of complexity and serves pedagogical purposes, must carry indicators that prove that the model is part of the reality with which it engages. It should also clearly indicate which reality—the reality of the observer—it refers to and where its points of reference are situated. This indication of connectability can be as clear as necessary and as diffuse as possible, in order to enable a maximum of diverse forms of subsequent communication. In synthetic cubism, the use of realia, sand, strings, nails and newspaper cuttings served as indicators of the reality of the observer. The model, however, can further approximate to the reality to which it refers, to the extent that there remains no doubt about the frame of reference and the kind of reality it engages with. In the act of transgression, it may attack those boundaries which represent the greatest annoyance of the avant-garde, that is, the boundary between 'art' and 'life'. And it may, with a degree of pedagogical urgency, place its concerns before the observer with such clarity that it risks losing its identity as a model. The model can approximate to reality to the degree that it becomes practically indistinguishable from the reality that it refers to. This is the case with many an interventionist, performative and participatory practice: in conducting interviews, in the compilation of statistics, the temporary assumption of particular roles, in the performance of certain activities, among others. In order to minimize the risk of not being able to differentiate between appearance and reality, and thus of mistaking one for the other, the model is placed into a context which highlights its deceptive character. The instruments or the media of this distinction between appearance and reality are the gallery and museum spaces,[1] the stage, or the medium of exhibition within which the model is positioned. The context produces the differentiation between model and reality, which the model is not in a position to achieve with clarity, because it tries to formulate

---

1 Brian O'Doherty, *Inside the White Cube: The Ideology of the Gallery Space* (Berkeley: University of California Press, 1999[1986]), p. 65 ff.

its exemplificatory content so clearly that it risks being practically indistinguishable from that which it refers to. And becomes redundant. Precisely because facts are to be delineated as clearly as possible, the model blurs the difference between itself and that which it represents, the difference which has enabled the production of meaning in the first place.

The second method which art uses to respond to the possibility of freedom and redundancy after the end of art is that of the production of complexity. The work of art becomes a self-referring absolute without reference to anything outside it. All lines of reference are either thinned out or cut off. There is no attempt at dealing with the question of offering a justification. The heteronomous, with which the work of art could have a certain equation, is not offered as a supportive context. What is then produced as a work of art is a construction of the highest complexity, one that bears and unfolds all references only as possibilities for more internal potentialities. What is taken from the world in the form of material, themes and methods is transformed within the work of art; contexts become more deeply intertwined, condensed, disentangled in surprising ways and reconnected elsewhere. Pedagogical concerns are as far from the work of art, which intends the production of complexity, as the will to accept moral restrictions or the responsibility for its effect. It reclaims a right to being as a thing among things, with a high degree of artifice; it drives out its own character as a fabrication, and, like the work that reduces complexity, it seeks to eliminate the difference between appearance and reality. It hypostasizes appearance as being equal to the real, because there are no other factors at play in it than contingency and arbitrariness. The work of art is a construction equal to reality, on par with it in its complexity and indistinguishable from it in its categorical status.

AFTER THE END OF ART

This kind of art tends to be under tremendous pressure in society. Art is the highly magnified improbability of successful communication. In the self-perpetuating process of diversification, in which it divides itself and splits up, art must attempt to reinforce its own value in all its manifestations. It must be in a position to do so for the whole of the system as its environment, and also for the subsystems that it divides itself into, if it is not to be replaced by other social practices. In the production of the morality of a context it can draw support from, over the last thirty years the art practices seem to have developed a strategy to compensate for the fragile justification of their own existence to continue in precarious autonomy as a realization of what is questioned and questionable in society.

This suggests an answer to the question: what happens after the end of art? Whether in the process of the reduction or production of complexity, whether through the exemplary conformation of sign and object or through autonomization at the expense of contexts, or the blurring or sharpening of the difference between appearance and reality (all of which amounts to the same thing), art produces morality. The end of art is the beginning of its return as morality.

The longing of art as moral praxis, the desire of art after the end of art is a desire for an imperative that neutralizes all centripetal and centrifugal tendencies, a desire for Nietzsche's 'law', a higher power, an ahistorical and timeless force under which all particular interests must be subsumed. The production of relevant contexts in the form of moral statements is supposed to relieve the work of art from its purely formal, purely 'aesthetic' disposition. The structure of diremption as the totality of the diktat to freedom must be cast aside by recourse to the ineluctable. Since the misery of the real world began to take shape, it is the longing for that point before time, the absolute beginning of the historical, that is crystallized in the concept of radicality as it is in no other comparable concept.

To a constantly diversifying society that is not able to master its own diversity, the paradigm of radicality, which in its compactness is a counter image of existing complexity serves as a corrective to an increasingly unmanageable reality.[1] From the realm of the political, in which the expression had been

---

1 Symptomatic of this was the 7th Berlin Biennale. See Artur Zmijewski, Joanna Warsza, *Forget Fear* (Cologne: Walther Konig, 2012), p. 13. Even worse, documenta 14, curated by Adam Szymczyk.

situated, 'radicality' simultaneously drifts into the realm of the aesthetic, that is, into the business of art. There it can function as a key concept set against the contingencies of social processes. At the same time, it is politically neutralized and aesthetically valorized.

The discourse on radicality is primarily the production of relevance in the face of a nearly boundless permissiveness of societies, which seeks an unrestrained capitalization not only of services and commodities, but also of values. On the one hand, the modernist paradigm of the opposition between art and society that is coming apart at the seams is looked upon as no longer appropriate yet indispendable should the players in the subsystems of art wish to insist upon its insubstitutability. For this reason, the discourse on art has to be pumped full with the force of the radical as a compensatory surrogate. The term uses the heft of the utopic pathos of modernity in order to compensate for the real shortcomings of art which is incapable, and rhetorical deficient, at presenting a relevant commentary in the face of a highly complex reality, let alone initiating change. Radicality implies a return to and unveiling of a truth buried or corrupted over the course of history. Radicality implies last truths, the certainty of which cannot be diminished. The discourse of the radical with respect to contemporary art is proof for the hypothesis that the Western concept of modernity (and thus also the idea of the post-modern) along with the Western notion of the progress of art are dependent upon a conception of history that must be read as a history of profane salvation.[2] The

---

2 See Karl Löwith, *Weltgeschichte und Heilsgeschichte*, VOL. 2 (Stuttgart: Kohlhammer, 1983), p. 223: 'K. Immermann correctly observed that the excessive political radicalism which characterises all the great movements of occidental history since Charlemagne, has its actual origins in the radicality of the Christian message, that it remained unknown to the sharpest

desire to find the blackness in black, the squareness in a square, the colourness of colour, the radicality of the radical, and with that, to have found the very end and therefore also the beginning, which are ineluctable, is secularized eschatology.

The path to salvation must be shortened through recourse to a hypothetical intrinsic authentic, to the 'primordial',[3] which corresponds with the prospective. In the desire to suspend diremption, and insofar as it conjures up an utopic-aesthetic radicality (Buchloh),[4] the discourse around contemporary art proves to be retrogressive. Creating a community becomes a way to put an end to the fragmentation of society into a multiplicity of milieus. What is imagined is a premodern state of unity and common interests and of shared direction of historical movement, as though a return to the tribal could provide an escape from the malaise of modern, functionally diversified society.

That radical art should be in a position to reach into an area which, as a sphere of the primordial, the elemental, the true, lying just below the horizontal interconnections of the present, is indicative of a conception of art which is related to

---

crises of antiquity.' See also John Gray, *Al Qaeda and What It Means to Be Modern* (London: Faber, 2003), p. 103: 'The prevailing idea of what it means to be modern is a post-Christian myth.'

3 Heidegger's reference to 'primordial thinking' is of course similarly tethered to the future. Those who know how to think 'primordially' also know how to think 'prospectively'. 'The world-historical thinking of Hölderlin that speaks out in the poem "Remembrance" is therefore essentially more primordial and thus more significant for the future than the mere cosmopolitanism of Goethe.' See Martin Heidegger, 'Letter on Humanism' (Frank A. Capuzzi trans.) in *Martin Heidegger: Basic Writings* (David Farrell Krell ed.) (New York: Routledge, 1977[1949]), p. 219.

4 Benjamin Buchloh in Isabelle Graw (ed.), *Texte zur Kunst* 81 (March 2011): 80.

Nietzsche's 'distant sensations' and to his hope that art, and the work of art as a soteriological machine,[5] may be able to achieve what was hitherto not possible in false reality—the salvation of the human being. This kind of liberative art is an art of rapture, an art that reactivates the past in the present and the potentiality of a buried authentic. The unearthing of roots is an excavation of the depths in order to reveal a point of origin which has after all only been buried over centuries of misled praxis by way of which occidental society grew away from its true purpose. It does not matter in the least that that point of origin may never be found again. Over the course of three steps, namely, the primordial state, historically occurring decadence, and ultimate rescue as a bending backward of history to its origins before it was history, radical thinking corresponds with the Christian pattern that Vasari's model of history had followed. In this case also, the validity of Löwith's thesis proves true, that radicalism is the profanized history of salvation.

The paradigm of art as rapture plays an important role in the first half and in most manifestations of the second half of the twentieth century. One needs no reminder of the Munich and Dresden Expressionists, the Fauvists, Brutists and Dadaists, the Surrealists, the gestural abstraction of the Tachists, the Art Informel in Germany, abstract Expressionism in North America, Viennese Actionism and the somewhat (already anaemic) case of the Junge Wilde movement. In their preference for the ecstatic as opposed to the calculated, planned and studied, all these forms of art are in search of a conjunction of contemporaneity and timelessness, momentariness and trans-historicity. It is an art of forgetting, and this forgetting is essentially one of the effects or tricks taught in the academies, those incubators of a

---

5 Giorgio Agamben, *Die Zeit, die bleibt. Ein Kommentar zum Römerbrief* (Frankfurt am Main: Suhrkamp Verlag, 2006), p. 96.

poisoned art of the cultural.[6] Art as ecstasy is always anti-civilizational and anti-cultural.[7] It rejects the present as misguided and malformed, as aberration or perversion, and in its place proposes an art before its times, an art for which the barbaric and the savage are a symbol. Like in Freud's *Totem und Tabu* (1913), she is considered the child of human history, whose actions and creations represent the same kind of purity, originality and innocence that is attributed to the actions and creations of a child.

These conceptions of ecstatic radicality have since themselves become historically determined before the figures of speech of radicality could have been exhausted. Moreover, radicality is one of the most common currencies with which to contrive relevance in the art discourse. However, now it is tethered to the idea of community as a utopic form of human sociality.

In 1924, Helmut Plessner argued that 'industrialism is the form of communication, expressionism the art form, and social radicalism the ethics of tactlessness'.[8] And: 'Tact is the entirely genuine and eternal respect for the other soul, and therefore the first and the last virtue of the human heart; from respect for one's own individuality and that of the other follows the most important symptom of tact: tenderness.'[9] Plessner's critique of the ideology of community works with the necessity of masking,

---

6 See Werner Hofmann, 'Die Kunst des Verlernens' in Jonathan Fineberg (ed.), *Kinderzeichnung und die Kunst des 20. Jahrhunderts* (Stuttgart: Hatje Verlag, 1995).

7 For the detailed theoretical framework of the anti-cultural, see Jean Dubuffet, *Prospectus et tous écrits suivants*, VOLS 1 and 2 (Paris: Gallimard, 1967); VOLS 3 and 4 (Paris: Gallimard, 1995).

8 Helmut Plessner, *Grenzen der Gemeinschaft* (1924) (Frankfurt am Main: Suhrkamp Verlag, 2002), p. 110.

9 Plessner, *Grenzen der Gemeinschaft*, p. 107.

of role-playing in public to protect from hurt and avoid pain. In interacting with others in the public sphere, the human being is not in a position to constantly bear the force of honesty. The morality of honesty turns into inhuman terror, which takes individual inadequacies as cause for brutal critique. Plessner associates the critique against the terror of community with a critique of the soullessness of the hounded man-machine[10] who has no time to perceive or take into account the nuances in the behaviour, wishes and feelings of their counterpart.

Tact as respect for the other is respect for that which is different. Tact and tenderness are in fact categories that can hardly be in consonance with radicality. Like community, radicality insists on agreement, one-dimensionality, closure and exclusion. Radicality cannot tolerate diversity in its conception; the radical is what is primordial and undivided, which suffered from division just like community, which figures as the coveted primordial, the elemental preceding an evil society.

---

10 See Helmuth Plessner, *The Limits of Community: A Critique of Social Radicalism* (Andrew Wallace trans.) (New York: Humanity Books, 1999), pp. 167–8: 'a materialistic view of nature; the stripping of soul and spirit from the organic body; the devaluation of natural phenomena and their simple standards for reality; an exaggeration that results from tearing the person's interiority away from its (objectual) bodily boundaries; purism, rigorism, and a hostility to the world contained in ethical principles; a fanaticism of ethical laws and a valorization of clarity; a pathetic parasitical commitment to unconditional authenticity in expression; and an exclusive validitation of unlimitedness. Whether capitalist or communist, such a person recognizes only the ideal, knows only values, and, where no value is to be seen, nothing counts as valid for him, nothing is worth doing. This person wants to have objective validity-what is recognized and translatable as such-at the foundation of his life. From his idealist position that norms should be realized for their own sake, he looks down with pride at the ethic of usefulness, at the morality of success, of expediency and of the greatest passion. But he is and remains only a pedant who having paid a price wants to be paid back in kind, no matter if it is with the heavenly manna of eternal values.'

Community includes who is similar. Community is based on the conformity of class, ethnicity, religion, gender, on a consonance of interests that call for representation. Interestedness is implicit in community. It constitutes itself as a positive abundance of shared interests that demand their rights. It needs no self-understanding or representation, since it stands in complete concurrence with itself. The dialectic of representation and absence[11] is cast aside in favour of a total presence. Community brings diremption to a standstill.

Communities that make a claim to rights insist on being regarded as part of a society that is based on a system of rights, and within and against which they struggle with other communities for their place in the realm of rights. Their right as a community requires no other provenance than that they consider it as their right as just and that they demand consideration. As generalizations of subjective rights, as a coupling of the subjective rights of the individual with the subjective rights of equals, communities represent a false form of general will, a generalization of individual will as collective will, which is directed not so much at the common good but at the advantage of the particular which one shares with equals and withholds from others.

Since community essentializes concurrence, it must hide difference within itself yet accentuate it more strongly on the outside as a difference from its other, from that which is different. For this reason, community produces its self and the other

---

11 See Hegel, *The Phenomenology of Spirit*, p. 342: 'This is so because where the self is only *represented* and *imagined*, it is not *actual*, and where it is *by proxy*, it is not.' See also Carl Schmitt, *Verfassungslehre* (1928) (Berlin: Duncker and Humblot, 2003), p. 243, in which he refers to Rousseau's argument that 'the people cannot be represented. They cannot be represented because it must be present, and only that which is absent, not present, can be represented.'

in a permanent process of constituting itself as substance.[12] The self only comes into existence in a rejection of the other, as a difference of predicates such as religion, skin colour, ancestry. It is in this production of difference that the violence of the social form of community lies.

At the same time, it is important to accurately describe what form of difference is being produced by community. It is a difference in view of the value of substance, through which community defines itself with relation to the other. The substance that binds members of the community with one another represents a value in itself, and it does so irrespective of any comparisons. Its value is contained in its regard for community, and the fact that community 'owns' this value through which it constructs its identity justifies the claim that this estimation of its value be regarded as a right. Little as the values that require no comparison, no further derivation, no discursive mediation, equally little are the rights in need of a further justification that rests on the value as substance. These are rights as rights, an extension of the basic form of human rights, of the subjective right to have rights. They are rights by virtue of their exclusion of other communities and its members from the same set of rights. The amalgamation of the claim to a consideration of abstract rights with the essentialization of this right produces the difference, which is as crucial as it is overlooked, but on the basis of which distinctions are made without comparisons. Such difference produces right as the universal that is withheld from the other as particular. Rights do not require any other justification than that one simply has them. This means, they rest on

---

12 See Jean-Luc Nancy, *Die herausgeforderte Gemeinschaft* (Zurich: Diaphanes, 2007), p. 30. See also Claude Left, 'Die Frage der Demokratie' in Ulrich Rödel (ed.), *Autonome Gesellschaft und libertäre Demokratie* (Frankfurt am Main: Suhrkamp Verlag, 1990), pp. 281–97.

the violence of assertion. Produced in the course of forming a community as a community by equals, this violence is directed not only at the other on the outside but also against the emergence of difference within. The efforts of a community towards constituting itself can also be described as efforts to identify difference that must be erased. Both within and on the periphery, these efforts produce an Other in order to obliterate it so as to produce itself in its sheer positivity.

The difference that establishes a community is not a formal difference but, rather, a difference of value. This value is an identarian one, which promises the possibility of self-constitution and has immunized itself as unassailable. To question it would mean calling into question the worth of the subject that demands consideration of this value, and the value of the community of subjects that define themselves together through this value.

Community produces violence, it marks out territories of non-communication. It cannot be compared with community in the sense that Kant means it when he writes about *sensus communis*. This sense of a collective, a shared sense of community, is produced through a comparison of judgement arrived at—and lost—in the process of reflection, in the comparison of what is established on doubt as foundation and exposes itself to the peril of vanishing; unless the possibility arises to build this community on the fragile foundations of commonality as a fragile concurrence. Such a community is based not on qualities such as colour of the skin, on religion, or ethnicity, but on the collective use of reason.

It may be that Plessner's 'tact' and 'respect' cannot be compared with Kant's 'consideration'. Yet, even if they are ordered along different registers, they are not very far from one another. As unlikely as it may be, the consideration for all of human reason relieves the subject of the limits of her private opinion, and demands an acknowledgement of the contradiction that it can experience, by way of comparison, as a shaking up of its self-certainty as a subject.

It is only in the comparison of judgements and in the reciprocal ensuring of these rights upon the consideration of these judgements, that society is constituted, wherein its members are able to hold in high esteem the rights of others even when they run contrary to their own interests. They are masters of their rights insofar as they choose not to exercise them.

The association of the figure of speech of radicality with the image of community produces the heroism of militance that serves as a social glue to those that otherwise stand to profit from the permissiveness of liberal society. It provides art the aura of the engaged warrior, the vanguard, the engaged, which then can justify itself even when it is nothing but the embellishment of homes, since it reminds the citizen of her true purpose, which the merely beautiful often makes her forget.

Producing Truth / Morality

The ethical turn,[1] which follows the social turn in relational aesthetics and gives morality precedence over art, is currently the last observable phase of a specific history of art since Nietzsche, in which all hope lies in liberation through art, and the very existence of art is justified on the basis of this function. The demand often made of art is that it should take positions on problems which are tied to morality. Not only should art hold a particular morality, but also judge and comment on political events from an artistic-moral perspective, and through the respective constellations and situations it creates, it must propose solutions to overcoming social ills.

How should one then imagine the relation between art and morality? What does art as morality do after the end of art?

Morality views the state of a social fact with respect to the good. The work of art also counts as a social fact in its dual character as a socially determined autonomous and a social.[2] Autonomy is not understood as autonomy from society but, rather, as a 'release for a specific function [. . .] as the realization

---

1 See Claire Bishop, *Artificial Hells: Participatory Art and the Politics of Spectatorship* (London: Verso, 2012), p. 18.

2 Adorno, *Aesthetic Theory*, p. 312.

of society [. . .]. Art shares the fate of modern society precisely because of the fact that it is trying to find its feet as a newly autonomous system'.[3] In being released within society as autono-mous, art is embedded in the totality of the social, and thus represents a legitimate object of moral judgement. The scope of morality as a form of communication cannot be limited in any society of which art is supposed to be a part.[4] There is no function specific to morality that would enable it to be limited to a particular area or subsystem.

The ways in which morality establishes an equation with art derive their justification from the idea that art is to be understood as social fact, and that for this reason, it can be seen in relation to the good. The attribution of value takes place on the basis of an assessment of the extent to which the work of art, precisely as a social fact, corresponds with the common good, affirms it or participates in it as the good in social processes. Morality identifies what is real in art as social fact in its autonomy, and determines its value in the form of a defining judgement. It is the purposefulness of a social fact, in this case the work of art, that is determined with respect to the good as purpose.[5]

Morality judges the work of art on the basis of its propositional content, on the basis of what could be communicated in the form of a text, and which is usually classified as content. (For instance, Christ as a crucified frog.) It views the work of art in its referentiality with respect to a reality outside of art, and, in that process, examines whether this reference corresponds to conceptions of the moral and the good or conceptions of the true

---

3 Luhmann, *Schriften*, p. 142 (emphasis as in original).

4 Niklas Luhmann, *Die Moral der Gesellschaft* (Frankfurt am Main: Suhrkamp Verlag, 2008), p. 336.

5 Kant, *Critique of Judgement*, §15, p. 44.

and the right, whether the work of art participates in the production of the common good or in the production of truth. Even where there is no propositional content (monochrome blue surfaces, empty spaces, a hole in the ground), the relationship to reality continues to exist. One could argue that in the rejection of the representative function, or of mimesis, lies a rejection of observable reality, which morality takes hold of in order to subject it to judgement. The morality of the a-propositional work of art would lie in its rejection of morality or represent a kind of über-morality beyond the moral. The production of art that is not required to demonstrate propositional content and cannot be used pedagogically can be read as defeatism in the project of raising the new human race or as heroism of abstraction, of the belief in pure form, as a brilliant spiritual performance or anything else, depending on which statements of the author are available, and which discourse—for instance, those that celebrate abstraction as freedom, or those that denounce it as mere formalism—has developed as the dominant one.

One side or other always tends to argue with one or other of these moralities in the defence of one or another kind of art. The art discourse has offered and continues to offer a range of possibilities to moralize against morality[6] and to selectively point out the stupidity of the evil or the virtuous,[7] and to

---

6 Luhmann, *Die Moral der Gesellschaft*, p. 336f.

7 See Hegel, *The Phenomenology of Spirit*, p. 224–5: 'The way of the world is victorious over what constitutes virtue in opposition to it. It is victorious over that for which the essenceless abstraction is the essence. However, it is not victorious over something real but only over the creation of differences which are no differences, over this pompous talk about what is best for humanity and about the oppression of humanity, this incessant chattering about sacrifice for the good and the misuse of gifts.—Those kinds of ideal essences and purposes all slip away from sight since they are only empty words which elevate the heart but leave reason empty; they edify but erect

demonstrate to respective opponents that they are trying to dismantle the morality of others with the help of moral argumentation.[8] Moralities function as boilerplates of what is termed art criticism or art discourse. They travel as freely available bots through the operating system of art, in which, depending on the need, they can dock at one or other stylistic preference or one or another praxis, and unpack there. The largest proportion of art has been and continues to be a commodity. That it simulates an added intellectual (and possibly also aesthetic, spiritual, ideological, etc.) value is integral to the commodity. The conviction that a work of art transports this 'added value' resists all doubts and better insights. Even the denial of this 'added value' through art can be read in the system of art as 'added value'. This is in keeping with the logic of the system that it cannot escape the re-entry of a fundamental differentiation. Art represents the highest stage of that development of capitalism in which the illusoriness of every value becomes manifest and must be concealed simultaneously. It is the purest form of the commodity, the exchange value of which has no relation to its use value. For this reason, it must produce the appearance of value—immaterial, intellectual, aesthetic, spiritual, cultural, religious, social, educative value and symbolic social capital.

What assembles itself as moralities around the work of art can fit any imaginable intention: critiquing the prices in the art

---

nothing; they are only declamations whose content is this: The individual who pretends to act for such noble ends and who masters such admirable oratory counts to himself as an excellent creature—he gives himself and others a swelled head, although the swelling is only due to self-important puffery.'

8 See Nina Möntmann, 'The Importance of Ethical Decisions in Participatory Art' in Nina Valerie Kolowratnik and Markus Miessen (eds), *Waking up from the Nightmare of Participation* (Utrecht: Expodium, 2012), pp. 193–7, for her attempt to morally discredit Santiago Sierra.

market as immoral, indignation at the injury to religious feel-ings, standing up for minorities, for the freedom of humankind, the rights of women, children, black people; denunciation of artists as charlatans and good for nothings, crackpots and tramps, provocateurs and parasites, attributing to them super-human abilities, glorifying them for their farsightedness and creativity, their sensitivity and subtlety, lauding them as embod-iments of the anti-bourgeois, and to idolize them for their uniqueness. Moralities are agreed on celebrating art as some-thing that differentiates human beings from animals. They praise art as soft power, as a medium of intercultural commu-nication, as the freedom and the laboratory of social creativity. They can judge art as socially inconsequential, as a feature of capitalist promiscuity in which even the most revolutionary instance in painting can become a suitable adornment for the Head Office of the CEO of XYZ company, and no avant-gardist experimentation with form is exempt from being turned into a design concept for a personal-care product or serve as a background for fashion photography.

Morality is necessarily defining. On the basis of normative assumptions about what the good actually is, the good of a social fact is extrapolated through a deductive process. The coin-cidental instance in its particularity and contingence is combined with the durability of what is normatively constituted and eval-uated on the basis of whether or not it corresponds with the superior good, and is defined as good or bad, good or evil.

The coexistence of different competing moralities indicates that morality is not exempt from the functional diversification of society. Needless to say that a sexual morality favours a dif-ferent good than economic morality. Morality finds itself to be self-contradictory when it is unable to judge the observable on the basis of a normative good, but has to develop it through the inductive process of observation. However, should morality not take this step, it splinters into a number of competing possibilities that cannot, even partially, be integrated but are instead exclusive. However, what they will not cease to do is to claim being morality. In its claim to represent morality, each of these moralities contains the great potential for violence.[9]

In splitting into a number of forms of moralizing, morality falls short of its own claims of functioning as a system free of diremption, and as one meant for the observation of society. Moreover, it also becomes clear that even though no particular area of application can be defined, morality claims that it is suited to functioning as a system of assessment of all social subsystems, to accommodate itself to them as objects of observation and develop suitable criteria for the description of the respective subsystem. What this shift from an observation of the second order into an observation of a third order equals, is the one from morality to ethics.[10] Ethics as a reflection of morality can observe when morality comes into play and with what justification [and for what reason]. While ethics as well does operate with the key differentiation between good and evil, it also offers the possibility of a turnaround, which morality is not in a position to reflect: the transformation of the good in morality into an evil. In view of competing moralities, ethics can let go of the decision regarding a defining and normative good and look for pragmatic solutions that do not rely on final justifications but tend to find the good in the consensual. Ethics

---

9 See Luhmann, *Die Moral der Gesellschaft*, p. 349: 'When one is on the right side of morality, there is little reason to make the effort to understand. In that event, all that matters is to aid the good towards victory, with ever more powerful means. Morality encourages rage.'

10 See Johannes Fischer, Stefan Grunde, Esther Imhof and Jean-Daniel Staub, *Grundkurs Ethik* (Stuttgart: Kohlhammer, 2007), p. 83ff.

as a process of reflection on morality decides on the good not as an observation of what occurs prior to this observation, but aims at the production of the good in the process of comparison between competing moralities.

As Though / Propositional Content / Morality

The work of art may be described as the production of the unity and coevalness of the binary of appearance and reality, as the production of the unity of that which has been separated through diremption, but held together by form. The work of art realizes itself in its dual nature as both illusory and real, as the unity of aesthetic difference which produces the simultaneity of appearance and reality in the form of the as-if.[1]

From this conjunction of reality and appearance results a relationality that unfolds in the work of art, a dynamic which produces a semantic surplus which can be described as a mode of mislaying of that which the work of art may refer to. In its idiosyncratic denseness in bringing together the contingent, in

---

1 Jacques Rancière, *Ist Kunst widerständig?* (Berlin: Merve Verlag, 2008), p. 27: 'Aesthetic difference is always to be produced in the form of the as-if.' See also Theodor W. Adorno, 'Extorted Reconciliation: On Georg Lukács' *Realism in our Time*' in *Notes to Literature* (Rolf Tiedemann ed. and Shierry Weber Nicholsen trans.) (New York: Columbia University Press, 2019), p. 223: 'In analogy to current philosophical expression, we might speak of "aesthetic difference" from existence: only by virtue of this difference, and not by denying it, does the work of art become both work of art and correct consciousness. A theory of art that refuses to acknowledge this is philistine and ideological at the same time.'

its formal consistency, and not on the basis of the representation of facts, the work of art possesses a kind of worldliness. There is always more to a work of art than is expected of it or it claims to have. It points to more semantic references than have been embedded in it intentionally. Its syntax—the ways in which the formal elements in the work of art refer to each other—is far too dense to be reduced to its propositional content. As long as it is in a position to create them, the chains of selection continue to exist over long periods of time, and change only when they are put to use in different historical, social, cultural and political contexts. Over time, the work of art becomes something more, something different; its context takes hold, and its self-constitution as aesthetic fact takes place in ways that constantly change.

When Nietzsche says, 'expecting an adequate expression is pointless: it is in the very nature of language, as a means of expression [...] to be only the expression of a relation',[2] he is expressing the inappropriateness of the demand that the work of art be an adequate representation of something outside of the work of art. What Nietzsche describes as means of expression is the medium of communication in which there is always more in circulation than what was intended. For the possibility of creating something new, and to communicate it, this surplus that exceeds the intention of the author, the polysemy integral to this communication is indispensable.[3] Meaning is the relation

---

2 Nietzsche, *Kritische Studienausgabe*, VOL. 13, p. 303.

3 See Maurice Merleau-Ponty, *The Prose of the World* (John O'Neill trans.) (Evanston: Northwestern University Press, 1973), p. 8, on 'the model of two thinking subjects closed in their significations—between them messages circulate which convey nothing and are only the occasion for each subject to observe what he already knew—and when the one speaks and the other listens, their thoughts reproduce one another, but unwittingly and never face to face.'

of the signifier to the signified, the way in which the signifier calls forth the signified and helps reveal it. Meaning oscillates as a tension between that which can be said and that which has not been said, that which is intended, and that which has been missed between unintended speech and that which is promised, the production of obscurednesses and the division of that which has been left to blindness through differentiation. This meaning, the signified, that which is referred to, does not precede communication. Rather, it is only brought into this world by it; there is no meaning before there is expression. According to Nietzsche, the reference to 'adequate means of expression' is not 'pointless' because expression goes beyond the signified, but because there is no object to which the expression refers, because the *adaequatio*[4] is a void that refers to nothing more than the autonomy of communication that brings forth what is signified in it.

The relation of expression is the relation of uncertainties that mutually identify and define each other in the process of communication. In the same way as the object receives its contour through the expression, it lends clarity, in its emergence, to the expression by which it has been produced. Uncertainty is thus constitutive of communication and is mitigated only temporarily through the clarification of relation.

Roman Ingarden writes:

For the participation of the work of art in the constitution of the aesthetic object, it is essential that it is a

---

4 See Martin Heidegger, 'Plato's Doctrine of Truth' in *Pathmarks* (William McNeill ed.) (Cambridge: Cambridge University Press, 1998), p. 168: 'And for a long time now in Western thinking, truth has meant the agreement of the representation of thought with the thing itself: *adaequatio intellectus rei*.'

schematic image, that is unequivocal only in certain respects while it simultaneously also contains points of uncertainly. Each of these points of uncertainty is a firmly circumscribed diversity of possible completions, of which only one succeeds in realising the transformation from work of art to aesthetic object.[5]

In Ingarden's concept of the aesthetic object which is not identical with the work of art, the aesthetic object emerges in the following three stage process: the material basis, which serves as a prerequisite to the work of art, which in turn represents the need for the constitution of the aesthetic object. Every shift from one step to another can be seen as a process of transformation or of translation, in the course of which the object, which is expected to receive a 'value-response', can change its position. Depending upon what notion of value it is subject to or offers itself up to, and in which context, the aesthetic object can assume the position of the work of art as also that of the bare materially present object to which absolutely no artistic value can be ascribed. As a result, it is the phenomena of the production of meaning and sense that accompany the journey of the object across the scale of varying attributions of value. In ways that cannot be foreseen, they constitute themselves as

---

5 Roman Ingarden, *Prinzipien einer erkenntnistheoretischen Betrachtung der ästhetischen Erfahrung*, Altes du IV-ème Congrès International d'Esthétique (1960) (Athens: Myrtides, 1962), p. 622f. Also, 'What is above all important is the differentiation between the elements of given circumstances in which aesthetic experience is possible. At the beginning of this experience there is (a) a work of art appearing against the background of a physical fundament, and (b) the one who experiences it. The direct interaction between the two leads to the constitution of the aesthetic object (c) as which the work of art appears. The interplay of these three factors produces an answer to the question of value (d), as well as the value-judgement that gives it its conceptual form (e).'

❀

AS THOUGH

the relation between object and observer in communication, and they constitute themselves exclusively as such and as being in the relation. The statements and judgements regarding value that are a result of the relation between object and observer, are the forms in which this relation is manifest. Inasmuch as the aesthetic object has been constituted through the assignation of value, they reveal its varying aspects which are inserted in the work of art as points of uncertainty or as the possibilities of the actualization of meaning. According to Ingarden, only in one sense is the work of art unequivocal, if at all, but in another sense it is of 'clearly limited manifoldness' in regard to the possible completion of the points of uncertainty and the actualization of their meaning.

It is the multiple stages in the constitution of the aesthetic object that imply its polysemy. The object of aesthetic observation can be seen as always only temporarily determinable if one understands the shift from one stage to the next, from material basis through the work of art to aesthetic object as the translation of the same object into different categorical conditions, in which meaning is simultaneously lost and produced, nuances are blurred and details accentuated anew, and meaning is drawn out of the depths into which it can sink. It then becomes clear what function aesthetics can have: neither the normative doctrine of beauty nor a science of sense perception. It is the observation of the attribution of values to social facts which are constituted as aesthetic objects for a certain number of reasons without remaining determinable as such.

The points of uncertainty that are germane to the work of art are phenomena of overlap, moments of semantic and syntactic compression and the consolidation of the idiosyncratic, the unification of the many-dimensional through form. These points of uncertainty are at the same time centres of energy, incubators for the transformation of meaning and sense, that themselves remain unchanged.[6] It is especially the syntactic consolidations, nodal points in a web of visual elements internal to the work that are of consequence. It is these syntactic consolidations that propel the autonomization of the work of art, as a whole, that is governed by its own laws without the need for external support.

The process of generating exemplificatory meaning serves the process of autonomization in an equal measure. Nelson Goodman[7] describes it as a process in which an exemplificatory case points to a label that denotes it. Both belong in the same measure to the spheres of appearance and reality and order themselves along the lines of aesthetic difference by way of the possibility of making reference. The exemplificatory case reveals what the label denotes, and both refer to a signified which does not appear in the reference system of exemplification but which is, instead, represented. The label denotes that which it refers to, like the exemplificatory case. Relatedness is as suited to the label as it is to the exemplificatory case; they are both about what they refer to. At the same time, it is only the label that denotes the exemplificatory case, and not the other way around. This is because the exemplificatory case cannot refer to the label, but only exemplify it. In the constellation of the exemplificatory case and label, differentiation along the lines of aesthetic difference—which the label, given that it can refer to the exemplificatory case—shares the illusory with the work of art, whereas the exemplificatory case shares with reality its status

---

6 See Luhmann's observation on form as unmoving mover, the theoretical implications (see Aristotle, *Met.* XII, 1072b25 und *Met.* XII, 1074b20) of which he does not follow through—*Schriften*, p. 207.

7 Nelson Goodman, 'Kunst und Erkenntnis' in Iser, *Theorien der Kunst*, p. 580.

as a mere mute object that can be referred to. This relation of 'aboutness'[8] is only possible when that which is referred to by both is not taken into account. As soon as it enters the frame of reference, the exemplificatory case changes sides and functions as that which is signified by the label and simultaneously, like the label, as the signifier of the signified, to which both refer. Thus it is centrally important that the respective positions of exemplificatory case and label and those of the silent signified along the lines of aesthetic difference are no longer secure and stable. In this field of relations, exemplificatory case and label are therefore temporarily the denoted and the denoting, signified and signifier, reality and that which denotes reality.

As long as the aesthetic object only ever constitutes itself, but does not exist, and in having constituted itself reveals itself as relational so that it is largely determined by the simultaneity of reality and appearance in having constituted itself, through consolidations that produce uncertainty by foregrounding meaning and reference, it is hardly possible for it to refer to a higher norm under which its value as good can be determined. It matters little which kind of moral norm comes into play, the object in its threefold form as material object, as work of art and as aesthetic object, and in its dual composition as reality and illusion, escapes every judgement. As long as morality has knowledge of the good—and it must insist that it does have this knowledge, if it is to be seen as morality and not simply opinion—that which eludes its judgement and its determination as good cannot be defined as good. That it eludes such judgement is a marker of evil, because the good is good insofar as it reveals itself as such to defining judgement from the point of view of morality.

---

8 Arthur C. Danto, *Die Verklärung des Gewöhnlichen* (1981) (Frankfurt am Main: Suhrkamp Verlag, 1991), p. 130.

The following could be a possible answer to the question regarding the relation between morality and art: the good cannot be identical with art, irrespective of the propositional content of the work of art. It is the platonic answer that damns the work of art, because it is appearance and therefore contrary to truth. Morality intentionally has to be about truth. It must claim the truth of the norms it has set in place, and must emphasize truth as the norm. Morality cannot solve the puzzle of the work of art. This is especially true insofar as the work of art cannot be negated?[9] While a statement can be true or false, its truth content can be confirmed or denied. This is not the case with works of art. A ballet, a poem, a pop song, a painting are not statements of which the truth content can be judged. A painting is never false, even if it is a kitschy imitation of a fifth-class representation of something dubious. The art and music industries, literature, entertainment media are, like all areas of social production replete with affirmatives, hollow and vapid garbage, hurried cobbled together and directed at rapid consumption, at the hurried satisfaction of urges. Their effect is meant to be brief, so that newer demand can arise. The art-crap which satisfies the retinal demands of the buying classes at art exhibitions is neither the production of lies nor of truth. It is rather the most conventionally mendacious placebo of the uniqueness which complies with the users' desires for social distinction. However, this is not about these forms of ubiquitous falsity as lubricants of social interactions, which is only too well known to most participants in the attention economy. This is about how the work of art, even the worst of its kind, in its dual constitution as that which is both real and illusory closes

---

9 See Jakob Steinbrenner, 'Bildtheorien der analytischen Tradition' in Klaus Sachs-Hombach (ed.), *Bildtheorien* (Frankfurt am Main: Suhrkamp Verlag, 2009), p. 285.

itself off to morality in eluding the possibility of its being negated. What cannot be negated is thus neither true nor false.

The work of art is thus not a method for the production of truth. It can neither be negated nor can it be said to be adequately describing something [a particular content], because the content that it is about is only ever revealed in the work of art. The work of art does not reveal a reality that lies outside it and to which it refers in the form of mimetic imitation or representation. Rather, it reveals its own methods of processing reality. This form of processing reality draws on its own ways of revealing reality as appearance and revealing appearance as reality in which it is to be located. The work of art can neither give up its claim to being rooted in reality, nor can it deny its own character whereby it belongs to the world of appearance. It is this two-facedness that represents its reality and the reality it processes. This also means that there is no realism in art because no reality that could have preceded its representation in the work of art can be spoken of. No reality that does not owe its existence to art can be isolated within art, irrespective of how fervent the attempts to take naturalism to its extremes and how impressive the effects of mimicry. The work of art is separated from the reality it is seen to refer to by aesthetic difference, which forces it to make as much space for reflexivity about its own mode of reality as its own reference to a heteronomous reality. The constitution of reality by the work is the processing of the heteronomous as the constitution of its autonomy. The work of art is attached to reality just like a membrane, upon which anything from the outside condenses in the same way as that which pushes outward from inside, like an expression which serves as the counter pressure to the impression of reality.

What reality is, reality cannot denote. However, reality does denote that which belongs to it, inasmuch as it is different from it.[10] The autonomous work of art, formulating its own laws, refers to the innate reality of its specific appearance. It reveals itself as part of a reality to which it belongs, making that which is not identical to it possible. A part of reality, the work of art emerges as something that is different from reality, and exemplifies what is contained in it and is seen as reality, as surpassing the excess of possibilities.

Adorno's description of the work of art as follows—'[I]n the context of total semblance, art's semblance of being-in-itsef is the mask of the truth'[11]—is motivated by his critique of the culture industry which seeks to conceal social reality with an insatiable illusionism.[12] The work of art participates in the production of appearance, in which it evokes an other as appearance, the illusion of the possibility of 'in-itselfness', as though there were something beyond the totality of appearance produced through the legitimacies of exchange and use. The appearance of 'in-itselfness' is the mask of the work of art, a duplication of delitescence. In this double delitescence as a seemingly twofold participation in the production of a social lie lies its truth, albeit not as truth that it would, by itself, be in

---

10 For a different emphasis, see Spencer-Brown, *Laws of Form*, p. 105: 'Now the physics himself, who describes all this, is, in his own account, himself constructed of it. He is, in short, made of a conglomerate of the very particulars he describes, no more, no less, bound together by and obeying such general laws as he himself has managed to find and to record. Thus we cannot escape the fact that the world we know is constructed in order (and thus in such a way as to be able) to see itself. This is indeed amazing. Not so much in view of what it sees, although this may appear fantastic enough, but in respect of the fact that it can see at all.'

11 Adorno, *Aesthetic Theory*, p. 227.

12 Adorno, *Aesthetic Theory*, p. 281: 'As semblance perishes in art, the culture industry has developed an insatiable illusionism. [...] The alley to semblance runs in counterpoint to its commercial omnipotence. The elimination of semblance is the opposite of vulgar conceptions of realism, which in the culture industry is the exact complement of semblance.'

a position to reveal but as truth about its social status. In the dialectic of appearance and elusion the work of art reveals its truth as a truth about its dual composition as reality and appearance. The way in which this truth about the work of art constitutes itself contributes to the system of art constituting itself as autonomous within society, as the realization of society. What emerges as irreplaceable is the specificity of observation of inherent difference, of a differentiation between appearance and reality that divides and separates reality in which appearance proves to be the truth about reality, and the reality of appearance speaks the truth about reality. Both these spheres are neither separated from nor bound to one another over the mechanisms of representation, of imagery or mimesis, but are deeply intertwined as they divide one another, and while dividing one another, they mutually produce each other. In this process, after a certain degree of consolidation, every trace of expression or intention is lost, and what is revealed is the pure relation as a generative force of signs referring to one another.

Along with the platonic one, this would be yet another answer to the question regarding the relationship between art and morality: morality as a form of defining judgement fails when it comes to art, not because art represents the realm of play, the domain of freedom, the sphere of inactionability, or for that matter any other fairytale world in which society wants to rid itself of its own burden, but because and to the extent that art as social fact not only eludes definability through moral judgement, but also eludes itself. It does not exist before a work of art has emerged, around which a discourse is built, which views, assesses and discusses it as aesthetic object. Art exists only insofar as the works of art that one classifies under it undermine the concept of art. Today, art as such exists only as something that cannot endure.

The missing out on art, as long as aesthetic objects are subsumed under it, on account of morality is not a failure of art because of particular morals. The failure of morality, which is apparent in the multitude of parallel forms of morality all claiming moral weight, is the failure of the multitude of individual wills, aggregating themselves to a false collective will, an expression of latently violent universalization of the particular, a symbol of the lapse into the appearance of positivity. Art after the end of art, the art of morality, shares the fate of failure with morality. It is the art that moves inexorably to its end, in which it attempts an amalgamation of art and life, the erasure of aesthetic difference, unable to stop being art; in Hegel's words, romantic art 'is the self-transcendence of art but within its own sphere and in the form of art itself'.[13] It is the art that seeks to be rid of its character as illusion, art that wishes to be reality. The blurring of boundaries in the arts results in a continuing conceptual expansion as well as a pushing of boundaries, an endlessly perpetuated sequence of transgressions after which art only comes back to itself as though it were simply a persiflage of the promise of beauty that can only be realized in the future, the promise of a happiness that will never come.

---

13 Hegel, *Aesthetics*, p. 80.

Aesthetics and Interest

The end of art as the end of the necessary appearance of truth in beauty marks the end of aesthetics as the science of sense perception and as a normative doctrine of beauty. It bears reiteration that, in being a part of culture as a system of observation,[1] aesthetics can be described as a process which observes the attribution of values to social facts, which for a certain number of reasons are constituted as aesthetic objects without having to be permanently characterized as such. Aesthetics describes the oscillation of social facts between material and aesthetic object, the migration of one and the same social fact through the space occupied by social values and making them comprehensible by providing reasons. It does so as a descriptive process in order to communicate to society—in which the attribution of values and the observation of this attribution takes place— the meaning of what is unfolding within it. Aesthetics is a system of observation with the help of which a society attempts to seek clarity on why and under what circumstances which attributions of value take place, which constellations ease or hinder, enable or inhibit, what kinds of other-than-artistic conditions,

---

1 Dirk Baecker, 'Arbeit an der Kultur' in *Wozu Kultur?* (Berlin: Kadmos Kulturverlag, 2012), p. 82.

THE ART OF DIREMPTION

forms of communication and discoveries call for the valorization of objects as aesthetic objects or as the end of art. In that
sense, aesthetics is both art history and the theory of art, history
of form as well as style, social history of art and iconography,
visual culture and iconology, semiotics and iconicity, and so
on. It synthesizes the propositions and results of individual
methods in order to write a history of the 'economy of values'.
This synthesis takes place as a diachronic examination along
historical lines and as a synchronic view in order to represent
the simultaneities, overlaps and discrepancies, and identify com-
plementary as well as contradictory tendencies in various geo-
graphical, social and political spaces.

Nietzsche's revaluation of appearance and his rejection of
the differentiation between beauty and ugliness (ugliness is not
to be found in art) places a certain burden on art. It represents
the strongest transformative force and the law under which the
human being 'does away with' herself. Since Nietzsche, art has
to be viewed in terms of its relationship with life. The differentiation between reality and appearance is the key differentiation
in aesthetics, which observes ways in which art processes this
differentiation, which is identical with aesthetic difference, in
the work of art. Should it wish to do justice to the art with
which it is concerned, it must see differentiation between reality
and appearance as a description of the border, on which art
reflects about its own status, that is, on which it is decided what
art is. The ways in which different kinds of art ascertain their
relation to their being art is revealed at this border. And at this
stage in the process of forming the aesthetic object, art may
establish itself as autonomous, as a system of decisions that can
be found again within itself as reflections of these decisions.

The relation of art to the world may be denied, the reference to the world may be obfuscated, perceptions about its

boundaries can be negated. The insistence upon an older concept of art, one that is not formulated along aesthetic difference but along the differentiation between beauty and ugliness, the preference for construction and the preference for the expressive, the direct impinging upon social processes through intervention and participatory art such as denying the very character of art through art itself—all these can be seen to be as much of a reference to the question of the relation of art to the world as the offensive avowal of the transgression of all its boundaries towards the world. Art does not have the option to reach back to a status prior to the paradigm shift that is associated with Nietzsche.

However, this only marginally affects the freedom of the observer to attribute certain values to aesthetic phenomena that can be classified under the paradigm of aesthetic difference. The user of art is free to choose a bunch of flowers instead of a lump of fat in the corner or a lecture in place of an idyllic landscape, and to give appearance precedence over reality or to give reality a place higher than appearance. Aesthetics observes this attribution of value, it observes the relation that the aesthetic object has to the aesthetic difference inherent to it. Its interest is governed by the object's reference to the division characterizing it and by the question as to which values are a part of the reference to this division by society in which the work of art exists. Aesthetics does not try to tell the truth of the work of art, because the work of art does not produce truth. It does attempt, however, to tell the truth about the work of art. To the extent that the truth about the aesthetic object is the truth about its social status, aesthetics, which observes this social status, is the attempt at the production of a truth.

The truth about the aesthetic object is thus the truth about its social status because it constitutes itself through its relation to reality. And this reality is the reality of society, because no observation is possible outside communication, and therefore outside society. The work of art does not constitute itself as sculpture, painting, piece of music, poem, or any other form. Art can, after the end of art, appropriate all kinds of contents and materials, objects and media, these criteria for defining art are far too arbitrary and unspecific to enable one to speak about what the aesthetic object is. The only thing that distinguishes it is aesthetic difference in the form of the as-if as its relation to its reality as appearance and to reality, and both reality and appearance are both communicated as being socially observable, as something that circulates in communication.

As a system of observation, aesthetics cannot escape the dilemma that the observed manifests itself in the process of observation, that the validity of the observation results from the fact that observation produces its object. Plausibilizing the validity of outcomes is a result of the autonomization of the system through the copying back of the differentiation into the differentiated; through autopoetic closure. In that sense, aesthetics follows an interest. It is directed by a singular interest in its self-plausibilization through evidence of agreement between observation and its object, and it is interested in defining the aesthetic object as undefinable, as a unity of the different and of diremption in its dual form. The interest in defining the object is the interest in speaking the truth about the object. Aesthetics is interested in its purposiveness with a view to participating in the production of truth.

Since the end of art, the relation to the aesthetic object has been one divided within itself, since what the aesthetic object 'arouse[s]' in us by works of art is not just immediate enjoyment but our judgement also, since we subject to our intellectual consideration (i) the content of art, and (ii) the work of art's means of presentation, and the appropriateness or inappropriateness of both to one another.'[2] After the end of art as the emergence of truth in beauty and the differentiation between modes of representation, reflection disintegrates into the observation of form and substance, in the differentiation between modes of representation and content. The end of art is also the end of the approach to art that Kant had described as disinterested pleasure. It is not only aesthetic objects that refer to the historical and social status of beauty. This reference is made, in fact to a far greater degree, by reflection about aesthetic objects, as aesthetics serves society to understand its own systems of attributing value. As mentioned earlier, value is not only that which proves itself to be useful, thus claiming a certain price. Rather, values are the result of interests as relations between objects and their observers.[3] Those who speak of aesthetic values, also speak of interest in the aesthetic object (which is not a manifestation of beauty, but a manifestation of diremption) and of interests that a society seeks to satisfy through the given object.

---

2 Hegel, *Aesthetics*, p. 11.

3 Benbow Ritchie, 'The Formal Structure of the Aesthetic Object', *Journal of Aesthetics and Art Criticism* 3(11/12) (1945): 5–14, especially p. 5 f.

The possibility that something new can come into being in the abundance and positivity of the world is rooted in the emptiness of aesthetic difference. What crosses the border between the realm of appearance and reality is transformed by aesthetic difference into something new. In that capacity, it produces a new experience in the realm of reality which the subject tries to process in the form of an aesthetic judgement.

In experience, what was till that point considered to be true is replaced by the object of knowledge, and by knowledge that must from now on be held to be true.[1] Experience suspends what is known. Not only does a work of art make a new experience available with respect to what it represents (monochrome blue surfaces, empty space, a hole in the ground, Christ as a crucified frog), it not only produces new facts, which may otherwise have remained unknown, it also presents as form a way of surpassing forms of thought about those facts. It makes the hitherto-unthought-of available to thought—that which could

---

1 Hegel, *The Phenomenology of Spirit*, p. 57: 'This *dialectical* movement which consciousness practices on its own self (as well as in its knowing and in its object), *insofar as, for consciousness, the new, true object arises* out of this movement, is properly what is called *experience*' (emphasis as in original).

❋

never have been thought of in the same way and never in any way other than this is revealed by the aesthetic object.[2]

Experience as a process of perceiving the new produces a new subject, not because the object of experience demands it but because experience itself as a suspension of what is known, as an event, in its formal emptiness, requires a reconstitution of the subject. The occurrence of the new produces a truth, and in puncturing the web of opinions,[3] it produces an immanent break. '"Immanent" because a truth proceeds *in* the situation, and nowhere else—there is no heaven of truths. "Break" because what enables the truth-process—the event—meant nothing according to the prevailing language and established knowledge of the situation. [...] We might say, that the process of truth *induces* a subject.'[4]

Should the experience of the new have set a truth process in motion (not every experience of the new necessarily does so, even when truth is the event of the appearance of the new),[5] the challenge is to maintain this truth by keeping it from being positivized or solidified, from being submerged in the web of opinions as the cement of the social beyond truth and falsehood.[6] What takes place in the event of experience must be understood as the production of emptiness. The 'punctuated' subject can

---

2 For a discussion on the concept of the 'unthought of ', see Max Imdahl, 'Giotto–Arenafresken', *Theorie und Geschichte der Literatur und der schönen Künste* 60 (1980): p. 91f. See also Helmut Kuhn, 'Die Ontogenese der Kunst' in Karl Oettinger (ed.), *Festschrift für Hans Sedlmayr* (Munich: C. H. Beck, 1962), pp. 13–55, especially p. 24.

3 Alain Badiou, *Ethics: An Essay on the Understanding of Evil* (London: Verso, 2012), pp. 42–3 f.

4 Badiou, *Ethics*, p. 43 (emphasis as in original).

5 Badiou, *Ethics*, p. 114.

6 Badiou, *Ethics*, p. 50.

uphold a fidelity to the event, which becomes its truth and to which it can hold on in the form of disinterested interest,[7] disinterested or devoid of interest because the interest in upholding the fidelity to the event does not equal the interest in the preservation, or even survival, of the subject as the bearer of the truth.

The positivization of the content of truth that must be valid for all and forever,[8] and the attempt of truth to assert itself is one of the forms of evil: 'The Good is the Good only to the extent that it does not aspire to render the world good. Its sole being lies in the situated advent [*l'advenue en situation*] of a singular truth. So it must be that the power of a truth is also a kind of powerlessness. [. . .] Every absolutization of the power of a truth organises an Evil'.[9] It is something good in its own right, that the truth that wants to do away with opinions and therefore needs to annihilate its bearers, cannot triumph.

When the subject has to reconstitute itself on the basis of the experience of the new, this experience, based as it is on the work of art, nevertheless takes place within the medium of the illusory, in the aesthetic appearance of the work of art, which only allows reflective, not defining judgement. The experience cannot be filled with positivity, the rupture that goes through the subject[10] cannot be mended by replacing purely formal communicability by that

---

7 Badiou, *Ethics*, p. 59, p. 85.

8 Badiou, *Ethics*, p. 27: '[A] truth is the *same for all*.'

9 Badiou, *Ethics*, p. 85.

10 See Adorno, *Aesthetic Theory*, p. 269: 'The subject, convulsed by art, has real experiences; by the strength of insight into the artwork as artwork, these experiences are those in which the subject's petrification in his own subjectivity dissolves and the narrowness of his self-positedness is revealed. If in artworks the subject finds his true happiness in the moment of being convulsed, this is a happiness that is counterpoised to the subject and thus its instrument is tears, which also express the grief over one's own mortality.'

which needs to be communicated, by trying to do away with the two-facedness of the aesthetic object and of the experience based in it with the avowal of reality. At the same time, the subject wishes to return to her interests; what was earlier truth becomes submerged in a web of opinions. Its necessary weakness is manifest in this disappearance of truth.

The figure of the interested/disinterested is analogous with the figure of the sublime in Kant.[11] The experience of the new, which also represents the convulsion of the self, its 'punctuation', gives rise to an interest in the truth of this experience against the sensuous interest, that is, against the subject's interest in her continued sensuous existence; an interest in affirming the truth is the estimation of an experience against every sensuous interest. It is an interest at the expense of interest in oneself. The aesthetic object, insofar as the subject exposes herself to its power, which may be capable of endangering its integrity, is a sublime one. It opens the subject to the possibility of her own existence, which goes beyond the possibilities hitherto known to her; through the means of art, the subject recreates herself beyond herself. However, this attempt to surpass herself is not a production of another, hitherto-unknown abundance and positivity, but the fidelity to the event demands that this rupture that goes through the subject, is maintained as a rupture, as a systemic void. It is up to the subject that has experienced this rupture to remain disinterested in her own existence and in how this rupture will be knit back together, filled up, be forgotten, closed, and healed. Disinterested interest is concerned with keeping open the aperture against all self-interest.

Insofar as aesthetics, like any other system of observation, is subject to interest, to the laws of an interest, which tries to

---

11 Kant, *Critique of Judgement*, §29, pp. 94–6.

demonstrate the plausibility of its process of observation by calling forth adequate objects, it finds itself exposed to the dilemma of the autonomization and the autopoetic closure of a system that calls for a corrective, an observation of a third order, so as to be able to prove its own plausibility in its environment. It is a question of the ethics of aesthetics.

The aesthetic object as a relation in its poly-dimensionality does not allow for a defining judgement, not because its beauty would permit nothing more than a subjective judgement, but because this poly-dimensionality and the arising uncertainties, the aggregation of contingence and complexity, ever allow only a temporarily valid statement about what exactly the object of observation actually is or consists of. It is the question of the existence of the aesthetic object and its temporal endurance within a particular order that does not allow for a defining judgement. In the truncation of the *adaequatio*, in the keeping itself open as a relation, as exemplification, in which signifiers refer to signifiers, the aesthetic object is simultaneously excluded from the possibility and relieved from the demand that it be a medium of the production of truth.

However, the production of truth is in fact the interest of aesthetics, and this is the truth about the social status of the aesthetic object in its dual form, both as appearance and as reality, the as-well-as, fragmented by aesthetic difference in the form of as-if. The judgement about the aesthetic object with a view to its social status is a defining judgement; it defines that which eludes definition as that which positions itself in relationship to the reality of the aesthetic difference in a particular way.

From the standpoint of the *adaequatio*, the aesthetic object is unrelated, and from the standpoint of relation only possible as a result of references. The interest of aesthetics is the upholding of the state of simultaneity of relatedness and unrelatedness of its object to the world. Insofar as the aesthetic object formulates an intentional relatedness to the world (as in the instance of participatory art), it is the task of aesthetics to clarify that this relatedness is a result of the effort to overplay its own fictionality without the aesthetic object being able to change its categorial status, by which it has been compelled to refer to appearance as reality and to produce reality as appearance.

Aesthetics is a reflection of the truth of the aesthetic object, a truth that resists its own hardening as a system, against the interest in self-plausibilization, upholds the interest in fidelity to the object in its interminable diremption and relativizes its own values with the insight that even these values are subject to the structure of diremption.

Such an aesthetics is appropriate to its object, to art after the end of art, to the art of morality, because it represents a moral practice in itself. It follows the interest of valuing the coupling of interest/disinterest as a central dual form of the relation of the object to itself and to its reality. To state it once again, values are a consequence of interests. The value of disinterestedness is a result of the interest in its continued existence in the form of an aesthetic object, as a form of reality, which, structured by aesthetic difference, enables the emergence of the new, divides reality itself into a particular and a general, into the incommensurable as the common feature of all objects that require a comparison, and in the incommensurable as that which can be understood in subjective judgement by a single individual as a particular, and is thus revealed as a disruption of the social, as a rupture in the horizontal fabric of opinions.

As a moral praxis that is in a position to define a 'good' for its own processes—fidelity to its object as an indefinable—aesthetics requires an ethics as a corrective that observes and evaluates its values. It is the task of ethics, and it is its due, to cast judgement on when aesthetics, in agreement with itself, can reason with the good that it has set before itself, and when it may defer to the intrusiveness of morality, tired of comparing its own judgements, weary of reflection, abandoning itself to the cacophony of opinions. An ethics of aesthetics observes when the good, which is defined by aesthetics, transforms itself into evil by submitting to the demand that the 'world should be turned towards the good', whether it is in the form of the imperative that art must fulfil one or other social function, to encourage criticality, to act emancipatorily, to contribute to the salvation, enlightenment, and freedom *et cetera* of the human being; or in the form of the juridical formulation of boundaries for what can be artistically permissible and morally acceptable.

Such directing of art towards specific goals from the view of which art can be seen as good or condemnable, constructive or corrosive, as contemptible or as admirable, as superfluous or necessary, is a form of the closing of the constitutive diremption of the aesthetic object in favour of a morality, which, given that it is conceptualized normatively, refuses reflection. Needless to say, morality necessarily fails the aesthetic object and is therefore inappropriate to it. However, the production of morality takes place not just outside of but within art itself, in the art discourse which masquerades as aesthetics although it does little more than bring together instances of the morally good, which then also circulate in society as aesthetic objects. Evaluating them, which is what casting a judgement about them is, falls to ethics as a system of observing morality to the extent that aesthetics makes use of it.

The Politics of Art

The use of morality in art has its origins in the overburdening of art as the great redeemer. Quite contrary to Nietzsche's intentions, a totalitarian moralization of art is the consequence. Inflated by moral fervour, the sweeping proclamations about art not only reek of arbitrariness, of which those who always intend the best without ever participating in the creation of the good,[1] are well aware, but also the fact that it fails its object; after all, the relevance of artistic practice and that of the accompanying reflection cannot be produced by doing away with the illusoriness of the work of art or by eliminating aesthetic difference and by attributing to the work the character of mono-semantically constituted realia, which should leave no space for doubt.

There is no telling what can be made of the aesthetic object. Unlike the concept of art, it is not a medium but a form, not a loose coupling[2] but an in-itself and for-itself necessary formation.

---

1 In this context, also see Hegel's ironic observations in *The Phenomenology of Spirit*, p. 358: 'Because the universally best ought to be put into practice, nothing good is done.'

2 See the definition of medium as used by Luhmann: Fritz Heider, *Ding und Medium* (Berlin: Kulturverlag Kadmos, 2005).

❈

THE ART OF DIREMPTION

Semantically overdetermined and closing itself off to both sides of aesthetic difference, on the basis of inherent uncertainties, it produces counter-sense as sense which reveals itself in time. It is on the basis of these uncertainties that it builds functionally short and ineffective, but in view of temporal availability, extraordinarily long chains of selection. Over the course of its availability, the work of art, which is unable to base itself on objective purposiveness, opens up various aspects to reflective judgement. It changes with time, and in the discourse built around the work of art and reflection about it—reflection as maintaining the division of the subject through the event of the work of art.

The event of the work of art does not create a new subject on account of the power that had taken a hold of the gentile Saul, but forces, albeit with relatively less violence, a new kind of subjectiveness based on the opening up and upholding the opening up of aesthetic difference that splits the work of art into spheres of appearance and reality. It is the separation that equally characterizes both the work of art and the subject, that the subject recognizes in the work of art, it is also separation that effects the dynamic that unpacks the work of art over time. Its autonomy consists in the ways in which it processes the heteronomous, how it integrates that which is alien to it into its own form, and integrates what is contrary to it into its own autonomous, sovereign construction. What works in the work of art is its inherent diremption unfolding within it.

This does not necessarily mean that a kind of effectiveness with respect to social, political, economic processes can be derived from such a construction of the work of art. The work of art is weak. As a work of diremption, it is slow, and it slows down further. This is not the case because it somehow, in some mysterious way in which art criticism refers to it, challenges entrenched habits or breaks conventions, but because the transition from one side of differentiation to another takes time, as does the retrieval of differentiation as content of the differentiated in the work itself. The way in which appearance conveys itself as more real than reality, and how reality in turn represents its illusoriness in the work of art that affirms its diremption, reveals it as absent, or rejects representation by insisting on the absent in appearance, understanding this constellation requires time and changes over time. What the work of art—on the one hand an instance of the reduction of complexities, and a fresh unfolding of parallel complexities and renewed production of complexities on the other—rejects in its idiosyncratic inwardness and by overplaying its own improbability, in its duality as both truly illusory and illusorily real, is the possibility of easily identifiable connections. Instead of opening them up, it closes them off, conceals and hides them, renders them unrecognizable, masks and veils them, and does so on both sides of the differentiation. A permanent failing of the character of the aesthetic object, a necessary misunderstanding, an inevitable going astray in the attempt at classification in the diverse registers of reality and appearance produces, on the side of the recipient, a failure of knowledge that reduces itself to categorization,[3] of judgement directed solely at certainty, bounces off from both surfaces, that of reality and of appearance. Just as the crossing of the aesthetic difference requires time, so does the processing of reflection in aesthetic judgement. The distancedness[4] of the work of art also requires the distancedness of ways of reflecting, that do not take into account the fact that reflective judgement as

---

3 Nietsche, *Kritische Studienausgabe,* VOL. 7, p. 498, p. 500.

4 Kurt Badt, 'Die Idee der Welt und das Sein als fundamentale Wesenheit bildender Kunst' in *Kunsttheoretische Versuche* (Cologne: DuMont Verlag 1968), p. 35.

unfoundable needs the painstaking and time-consuming comparison with the entirety of human reason in order for its validity to be tested. One of the readily practiced methods of reflection is the evocation of reflection, with the assertion that the work of art acquires its resistance through reflexive distancing from the social.[5] The elimination of the reflexive is a result of an easy localization of the quality of reflexivity on the side of a routinized and inconsequential unpacking of conceptual moments, which strengthens the cacophony of opinionation that art should somehow be critical. As it turns, the wheel of reflexivity produces what was a foregone conclusion: the claim of criticality, the production of new possibilities of connections to a further discourse which helps classify the work of art as a link in a chain of arguments, so that one can immediately forget all about it.

The relationship of society to the economy of values that it is responsible for having established reveals itself as being structured by a discourse of power, that insists on sucking up everything that is contradictory in a tyranny of a rationality aiming for monosemy. In this discourse, society remains blind to how, in the same measure that it produces positivity, it also produces appearance, which stands before reality as an inactive, useless, puzzling reflection that also completes it. In difference, in diremption, in the void of an empty gap, society has its counter-image. However, that appearance belongs to reality does not mean that both appearance and reality are dialectically 'mediated' by one another. They are not. The as-well-as of reality (and of appearance that comes with it) cannot be determined by dialectics: it is comprehensible as separation, as diremption, as both unmediated opposition and compatibility of interlocking

---

5 See Juliane Rebentisch, *Theorien der Gegenwartskunst* (Hamburg: Junius, 2013), p. 71.

and irreconcilable difference. This instance of the irreconcilably different as unity of difference is art that neither arbitrates in conflict, nor erases separation, but produces difference.

That art as an autonomous system participates in society as realization of the social is evident. However, does it also participate in politics as the self-regulation and self-governing of the social,[6] when it confronts power, which is the medium of politics,[7] in its weakness and powerlessness? And if it is the case that art rejects a conciliation with power, then what is it that it participates in as a realization of the social?

Art participates in the 'life in the polis',[8] it creates the public sphere as the space for the use of reason, a reflective and a sensibly behaved reason. It establishes the right of the subject, in that space in the public sphere, which should be a space of freedom and not a space of power, to speak as the subject that is the one as all.[9] Like any other truth, its truth holds true for all and for ever. Nevertheless, subjective right does not entail a general right that would be suitable for founding communities. Because, '[T]ruth is diagonal relative to every communitarian subset; it neither claims authority from, nor [. . .] constitutes any identity.'[10] The truth that justifies the right of the subject to not participate in the politics of power, is both individual and universal. What establishes experience vis-a-vis the aesthetic

---

6 Menke, *Kritik der Rechte*, p. 354.

7 Max Weber, 'Politik als Beruf' in *Ausgewählte Schriften* (Potsdam Internet Edition, 1999), p. 397.

8 Arendt, *The Human Condition*, p. 41

9 Menke, *Kritik der Rechte*, p. 362: 'It is only that process in which "one *as all*" can judge that is political; in which the merely particular and individual is overcome in the name of [in favour of?] collective judgement.'

10 Alain Badiou, *Saint Paul: The Foundation of Universalism* (Ray Brassier trans.) (Stanford: Stanford University Press, 2003), p. 14.

object (and this experience is always unique, individual vis-a-vis the individual, unique object), is this subjectivity which can be based on nothing but the event of truth. Truth is observation that can be plausibilized. It is the non-negotiable,[11] the substanceless, fragile, the untenable that is produced only in comparison as the possible, and only in its allegiance to it as truth; the baseless, on which judgement is based, the doubt that moves itself out of its way by proclaiming itself as its own fundament.

The attempt to turn the world towards the good can only be based on power. The good, based as it is on power, is revealed as a preparation for evil. The conjunction of art with the good is its powerlessness, a weakness that cannot be exorcized, an inability to change the world. Art relates to power as that which is separated from it, as a relinquishment of participation in power and as the use of the right of abstention that nevertheless both demands consideration and ensures it.

However, the politics of powerlessness is in no way akin to Franciscan humility. Politics of art as politics of powerlessness is counter-politics, it is the 'the appearance of men qua men in their distinctiveness',[12] it is the politics of free subjects in the process of producing themselves, incommensurable, unique, diverse.

It is a matter of a powerless insistence on the right of the subject to distance herself from communitization, from the totality; an insistence on fragmentation. It is this fragmented subject that develops, anchors, asserts and defends processes and methods, rules and rights, in the process of socialization as

---

11 Jean-Luc Nancy, *The Ground of the Image* (Jeff Fort trans.) (Fordham: Fordham University Press, 2005), p. 18: 'The intractable is always a mark of the truth.'

12 Arendt, *The Human Condition*, p. 176.

the production of agreement about the good by way of reflection as temporary stipulation. This can also be seen as the production of the right to not be harassed by politics, to be spared from being subject to totality, to be excluded from having to agree, to dwell in disagreement, to turn its back against society, to not wish for the good, not because one seeks evil, but because seeking to realise the good is itself evil.

A society that favours the discourse of power is the 'about which' of art as its own weakness. Art shows us how society eludes itself, in the process fictionalizing itself precisely where it seeks to be sure about itself. Society, in the discourse of power, produces the discourse of weakness as its own blind spot, as it fictionalizes itself and insofar speaks its truth about itself; it fetishizes power, not unlike art criticism that pretends to criticise it.

An ethics of aesthetics that is less concerned about the elimination of differences than it is about its production, that is less concerned about the phantasm of the reduction of complexities than about the reality of the production of contingencies, works on the self-description of society through the medium of art as a discourse of powerlessness. Such a discourse is the nucleus of a politics that places at its centre the utopian-nondisposable, that which separates itself, the groundless and irrevocable, the incommensurable. Democratic society constitutes itself by way of 'dissolving the basis of all certainty'.[13] It is a society of freedom as a society without a sovereign.[14] Insofar as this politics as the praxis of the political denies society a positive identification with itself, and maintains the location of power as a gap, it institutes

---

13 Lefort, *Die Frage der Demokratie*, p. 296.

14 See Jacques Derrida, *Schurken* (Frankfurt am Main: Suhrkamp Verlag, 2003), p. 104.

the rupture of diremption as difference between itself and its representation.

This founding of its own praxis as a founding on the unfoundable, as a questioning of the doubtful and as a fixing of doubt itself, as permanence of reflection without pause, binds the art that seeks to being something other than being merely useful to humankind, something other than the terror of totality, with a politics which discards the totalitarianness of community in favour of the permanent movement of its founding of society on its own insights into itself, garnered in comparison with all of human reason. If the political, in contrast to politics, categorically rests on nothing, when it only produces itself in its completion as a self-institutionalization of society,[15] without a preceding justification in rights or reason, as a power of the constitutive which subverts what is constituted and refashions it, only then can the work of reflective reason be considered to be an effort towards the political, as a working at democracy as an agonally composed public in which it is not power that makes the distinction, rather in the self-determination of society, it is the differentiation that surrenders the temporarily determined to the forever necessary deciding of the separate, its repeated separation and to its forever renewed determination.

Practiced in conjunction with the work of art, reflective judgement is political praxis as production of the public, in which the unfoundable singular, the rupture in the continuum of the social, in which difference, which maintains its weakness and powerlessness, and which is not reducible to any identity, extricates itself from positivization. The insistence on autonomy

---

15 See Andreas Hetzel, 'Vertrauen als Affekt der radikalen Demokratie' in Thomas Bedorf and Kurt Röttgers (eds), *Das Politische und die Politik* (Berlin: Surhkamp Verlag, 2010), p. 236.

of the work of art and the autonomy of judgement in self-determination, on the singular contemplation of the self-assuring subject with respect to the individual object as suggestive of all of human reason establishes the consideration of art as the political praxis of freedom.